"Clear, pragmatic, and lovingly optimistic, Vigil-Oten ... the tools and attitudes to stride confidently through thei ... al lives while being amply buffered against maturation  Delivering mindfulness and self-compassion practice ... mind, this workbook will engage and support teens in countiess ways."

—**Zindel Segal, PhD**, distinguished professor of psychology in mood disorders at the University of Toronto Scarborough

"Modern teens face a world filled with more social pressures than ever before. This clearly written book presents teens with a wealth of helpful guidance for building confidence and dealing with challenging life situations, skillfully drawn from cutting-edge therapy approaches. It then guides them to apply these skills to the common challenges faced by teens everywhere. Highly recommended!"

—**Russell Kolts, PhD**, professor of psychology at Eastern Washington University, and author of *CFT Made Simple* and *The Compassionate-Mind Guide to Managing Your Anger*

"This easy-to-understand and easy-to-follow guide for adolescents is a treasure chest of insightful and compassionate ways of understanding why our minds are the way they are, which helps us to reduce feelings of shame and build self-confidence. From mindfulness to assertiveness and positive relationship building, the authors offer invaluable guidance on how to work with our tricky minds and build confidence to pursue goals that are helpful to ourselves and others."

—**Paul Gilbert, PhD, FBPsS, OBE**, professor of clinical psychology at the University of Derby, visiting professor at the University of Queensland, president of The Compassionate Mind Foundation, and author of *The Compassionate Mind*

"Struggling teens benefit from clear instruction and guidance that promotes action. They also need to hear—over and over again—that their feelings, thoughts, and perceptions are not permanent, but instead are malleable and manageable. This book checks all those boxes: concrete, relatable, and full of steps that teens can use to build a more confident, active, evolving life."

> —**Lynn Lyons, LICSW**, author of *The Anxiety Audit*; and
> coauthor of *Anxious Kids, Anxious Parents*

"This caring, compassionate, and well-researched workbook offers teens an invaluable road map to build and rebuild their confidence. This workbook is packed with accessible mindfulness and compassion practices that are of ever-increasing importance in helping youth navigate the challenges and pressures of our current times. With engaging ideas and stories from their own personal and professional lives, as well as clear explanations of the best techniques the field has to offer, Vigil-Otero and Willard write like the warm, humorous, and experienced therapists they are."

> —**Joan Borysenko, PhD**, *New York Times* bestselling author
> of *Minding the Body, Mending the Mind*

the self-confidence workbook for teens

mindfulness skills to help you overcome social anxiety, be assertive & believe in yourself

ASHLEY VIGIL-OTERO, PsyD
CHRISTOPHER WILLARD, PsyD

Instant Help Books
An Imprint of New Harbinger Publications, Inc.

INSTANT HELP, the Clock Logo, and NEW HARBINGER are trademarks of New Harbinger Publications, Inc.

New Harbinger Publications is an employee-owned company.

The "Three Circles" model of emotions is adapted with permission from THE COMPASSIONATE MIND by Paul Gilbert, copyright © 2009 by Little, Brown Book Group Limited. Used by permission of Little, Brown.

The "Captain of the Ship" story in activity 13 is adapted from An Open-Hearted Life: Transformative Methods for Compassionate Living from a Clinical Psychologist and a Buddhist Nun, by Russell Kolts and Thubten Chodron, © 2015. Used by arrangement with Shambhala Publications, Inc., Boulder, CO. www.shambhala.com.

Copyright © 2023 by Ashley Vigil-Otero and Christopher Willard
                Instant Help Books
                An imprint of New Harbinger Publications, Inc.
                5674 Shattuck Avenue
                Oakland, CA 94609
                www.newharbinger.com

FSC
www.fsc.org
MIX
Paper from responsible sources
FSC® C011935

Cover design by Amy Shoup; Acquired by Jess O'Brien; Edited by Kristi Hein

---

Library of Congress Cataloging-in-Publication Data on file

Printed in the United States of America

25   24   23

10   9   8   7   6   5   4   3   2   1   First Printing

In memory of my dad, my winning ticket. Thank you for teaching me what matters most.

—AVO

With gratitude to my teachers and my students. I don't know who has taught me more. Their wisdom permeates these pages.

—CTW

contents

letter to the reader: how to use this book

Dear Reader,

Maybe you bought this book for yourself, or maybe an adult who cares handed it to you because they want to help. We understand that you're busy—with a social life, school, family, maybe even things like sports or a job—so reading and writing your way through all these pages is probably not at the top of your to-do list. Good news: You don't have to work through the entire book, cover to cover. Of course, you can if you'd like, and we don't mind if you do. But we wrote the book so you can skip around to focus on what matters most to you. You might choose to read on your own or with a trusted friend or adult who knows you well and supports you.

In our work as psychologists, we've found that when it comes to building self-confidence, mindfulness and compassion practices really seem to work well. Wondering why? We won't bore you with the research, but mindfulness, including practices of self-compassion, can help build inner resources for confidence and offer alternate routes around the most common blocks. Mindfulness in particular can allow us to see more clearly, providing helpful perspective and comfort when we most need it. And self-compassion can be key to resilience and self-worth, helping us recover from setbacks and more effectively work with that inner critic who tends to chip away at our confidence. (More on that later.)

Let's walk you through what you'll find in the book. Part 1 starts with understanding what self-confidence is, what gets in the way (the common blocks), and how to boost your confidence. You'll take some time to explore which areas of life you're already strong in and which are more challenging. From there, you'll learn about the automatic stress reactions that can worsen your challenges and undermine both your confidence and your resiliency, such as getting swept up by your emotions, avoidance, self-criticism, and shame. Although you *can* work through the book however you want to, we suggest you read part 1 first; it has core information and exercises that will relate to the other parts of the book.

In part 2, we focus on issues at school, walking through moments in a school day that are hot spots for confidence challenges, like talking to teachers, performing under pressure, and trying new things. Browse through these pages and see what is relevant for you. Try the specific skills and interventions for your personal hot spots, whether that's speaking up in class or dealing with academic upsets.

In part 3, we turn to social situations outside of school and how they affect self-confidence. Again, you can read in order or skip around to the issues that affect you most, such as dealing with worries before you get to a social event, navigating social mistakes, getting hurt, or feeling unsure in a relationship.

Throughout the book, we teach you things you can *actually do* to boost your confidence, manage your emotions, try new things, and recover from setbacks. We hope you find it helpful not just for your confidence, but also for getting you closer to the goals and dreams you're shooting for.

Of course, you might need more help than a workbook can provide. In fact, you may already be working with a therapist or counselor or talking to friends or mentors. Let us emphasize: there is no shame in asking for help. In fact, now more than ever it's common for teens to seek out therapy or counseling for all kinds of issues, small and large, and for either short- or long-term support.

We hope the practices on the pages that follow help you build on your current strengths and embrace a more confident journey, one where you can meet any ups and downs along the way with more grace, ease, and confidence. Let's get started!

—Ashley and Chris

Basics and Blocks

Part 1 starts by having you identify areas of your life that could use some extra confidence. We also want you to start thinking about what blocks your confidence, so you can better understand what holds you back and learn what you can do about it.

Although there are many possible reasons why people struggle with confidence, there are some universal barriers that can keep confidence low. This first section explores the most common barriers, starting with real-life setbacks—times in your life when you've failed or missed the mark in some way. These times happen to all of us and can often bring out intense emotions that hook us and ultimately undermine self-confidence.

Another common self-confidence block we'll explore is avoidance: a tendency to avoid the situations or experiences that challenge us. It's normal to want to avoid difficulty. But if you use avoidance as a life strategy, you tend to feed the difficulty and doubts— and you miss out on many good things in life.

The final blocks we'll look at include the inner critic and shame. Hearing a critical inner voice and getting lost in feelings of shame, believing you aren't good at your core—these will really do a number on your confidence and leave you feeling more stuck than empowered.

Do any of these blocks sound familiar? Do you have any other ideas of what blocks your confidence? If not, no worries; read on to learn more. Let's begin by diving into some essential information to help you better navigate common blocks and build up your confidence in spite of them.

1   unlocking self-confidence

for you to know

Self-confidence is based in believing you have what it takes to succeed and navigate obstacles that may get in your way. This is quite different from arrogance, where you might brag and come across superior to others. Self-confidence is also not about overestimating what you can do; rather, it involves having a realistic sense of your personal capabilities.

It's probably easy to imagine the many benefits of confidence: It can help you face pressure, take risks, tackle obstacles, and put others at ease. The harder part is figuring out what to do if you tend to doubt your abilities rather than believe in them. Then it can be helpful to know that confidence is not something you have to be born with. Confidence is something you can build on—and we'll help you do that with this workbook. Let's first address which areas of your life need the most attention; then you can identify goals to help you grow confidence rather than self-doubt and worry.

for you to do

What's your level of self-confidence right now? You may be more confident in some areas than in others. That's normal! No one is confident about everything all the time, no matter how they may seem to others. You could be totally confident on the soccer field but the thought of raising a hand in class makes you want to crawl under your desk. Take a moment to see where your strengths and challenges lie.

Consider your level of self-confidence in each area. Circle the rating that fits, with 1 being no confidence and 10 being complete confidence.

Social Life/Friendships

1	3	5	8	10
No confidence	Not very much confidence	Some confidence	A good deal of confidence	Complete confidence

Dating and Relationships

1	3	5	8	10
No confidence	Not very much confidence	Some confidence	A good deal of confidence	Complete confidence

Family

1	3	5	8	10
No confidence	Not very much confidence	Some confidence	A good deal of confidence	Complete confidence

School/Academics

1	3	5	8	10
No confidence	Not very much confidence	Some confidence	A good deal of confidence	Complete confidence

Sports

1	3	5	8	10
No confidence	Not very much confidence	Some confidence	A good deal of confidence	Complete confidence

Body Image

1	3	5	8	10
No confidence	Not very much confidence	Some confidence	A good deal of confidence	Complete confidence

Your Identity

1	3	5	8	10
No confidence	Not very much confidence	Some confidence	A good deal of confidence	Complete confidence

Arts

1	3	5	8	10
No confidence	Not very much confidence	Some confidence	A good deal of confidence	Complete confidence

Other Activities _____

1	3	5	8	10
No confidence	Not very much confidence	Some confidence	A good deal of confidence	Complete confidence

Test Taking

1	3	5	8	10
No confidence	Not very much confidence	Some confidence	A good deal of confidence	Complete confidence

Something Else? _____

1	3	5	8	10
No confidence	Not very much confidence	Some confidence	A good deal of confidence	Complete confidence

more to do

Look back at your completed survey. Star the items you want to focus on right now. As you work though this book, what are the specific areas of your life you want to target? What are your specific confidence goals at this time?

_____

_____

_____

What would your life look like if you were three points higher in each of these areas? Is there anything you would do more or less of?

_____

_____

_____

Can you think of what could get in the way of your goals?

_____

_____

_____

The remainder of this section will introduce core skills to help you build up your confidence and work with common roadblocks that often get in the way.

2   coping with setbacks

for you to know

It is easy to feel confident when we're winning. But we can't win every time. We all face setbacks and challenges sometimes—which can be opportunities for confidence to slump, or to grow. The secret to growth is in how we cope with what we face.

To boost your ability to cope with setbacks, an important first step is understanding your emotions a bit better. Dr. Paul Gilbert, who developed compassion focused therapy, created the Three Circles model of emotions to help us better understand our experience (Gilbert, 2009).

The Three Circles represent three systems that work together for our emotional regulation: the threat system (represented by a red circle), the drive system (a blue circle), and the soothing system (a green circle). Many of our clients have used the Three Circles to reset and take positive actions after a setback, which has been essential for their self-confidence. This matters because when we're stressed we might unintentionally make things worse—hiding from our problems, criticizing ourselves, or acting out. The Three Circles offers a helpful visual so you can shift out of stress and recover quickly with your self-confidence intact, rather than getting hijacked by your emotions.

THE THREE CIRCLES OF EMOTIONAL REGULATION

To help you visualize each system, color in each circle, using red for threat, blue for drive, and green for soothing.

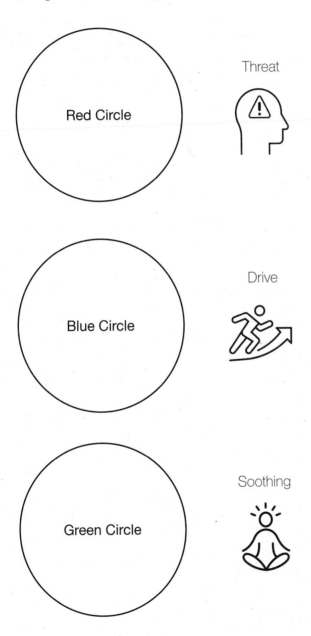

Threat

Purpose: To spot danger, warn you, and protect you when something isn't right.

Sometimes the threat system can take the job too seriously and go too far. If your red circle gets larger than the others, you are on high alert and may feel unbalanced. Threat emotions include anger, anxiety, fear, disgust, and shame. These don't always feel good, but remember, these emotions are just trying to help.

Drive

Purpose: To go after what you want and get stuff done!

The drive system can feel really good. The feelings here include excitement, interest, motivation, and aliveness. You may try to activate the blue circle to calm down the red circle. However, if your blue circle gets too big, you'll feel burned out and exhausted.

Soothing

Purpose: To help your brain and body slow down; to feel safe and socially connected.

The soothing system calms the threat and drive circles to create balance. Emotions include feeling calm, content, safe, and connected. Many people who struggle with confidence have a less developed green circle. Activating your green circle helps you shift out of stress.

7

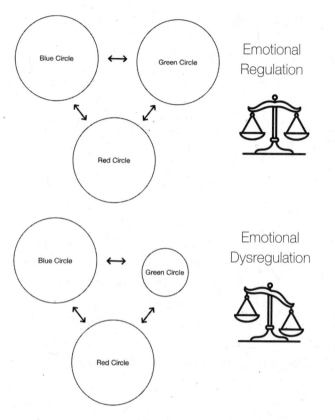

Emotional Regulation

The three systems work together to help you feel emotionally balanced. The more balanced your circle sizes, the more balanced you will feel. Recognizing when your red and blue circles are growing can remind you to activate your green circle for balance. When your circles are balanced, you can respond to life as your best self: confident, wise, and helpful.

Emotional Dysregulation

If one or two systems dominate, you'll feel unbalanced emotionally. With larger red and blue circles and a smaller green circle, you get stuck in a threat-and-drive loop that consumes your thoughts and emotions. This can leave you feeling out of balance, critical, and less likely to do something helpful.

Adapted from Gilbert, *The Compassionate Mind* (2009), modified with permission from Little, Brown Group.

for you to do

Knowing what circle you're in, and how your systems might be out of balance in any given moment, helps you find balance again. Read about how Ella used the Three Circles model, then answer the reflection questions that follow.

A few months ago, Ella received her score on the practice SAT. It was so much lower than she was expecting that she had an anxiety attack. She started studying to the point that she had no time for anything else. At first the extra work felt good, but over time it also tended to feed her anxiety. Eventually Ella's anxiety reached the point that she couldn't focus during her SAT study sessions at all. When she started therapy, her confidence for the SAT was at an all-time low and her anxiety and self-criticism at an all-time high.

Ella's therapist told her about the Three Circles model and asked her to draw her circles in relation to how she was feeling most of the time. Ella's red (threat) and blue (drive) circles were huge, while her green circle was just a dot. Drawing her circles helped Ella see that she was trying to manage the threat of low SATs with pure drive. She was caught in a threat-drive loop that was making things worse.

Now understanding what she needed to feel balanced, Ella shifted her priorities, scheduled more downtime, and learned how to grow her green circle. Outside of therapy sessions, the Three Circles model helped Ella notice when her threat and drive circles were taking over. She also learned that when she was harsh and critical with herself, her threat circle got supercharged. When she noticed her red circle getting larger, she learned to turn up her green circle with self-soothing skills like breathwork and by treating herself with understanding and kindness, as she would treat a friend in need of support.

Over time, Ella's circles balanced, which helped her studies, mood, and confidence. The next time she took the SAT, her ability to cope with the pressure improved, as did her actual score.

How do your circles stack up? In the box on the left, use colored pens to draw your circles in proportion to how you currently feel most of the time. Use red for threat, blue for drive, and green for soothing.

Then, in the box on the right, draw your circles as you would like them to be in the near future. Which of your circles might be a bit too big right now, and which ones could stand to grow a bit?

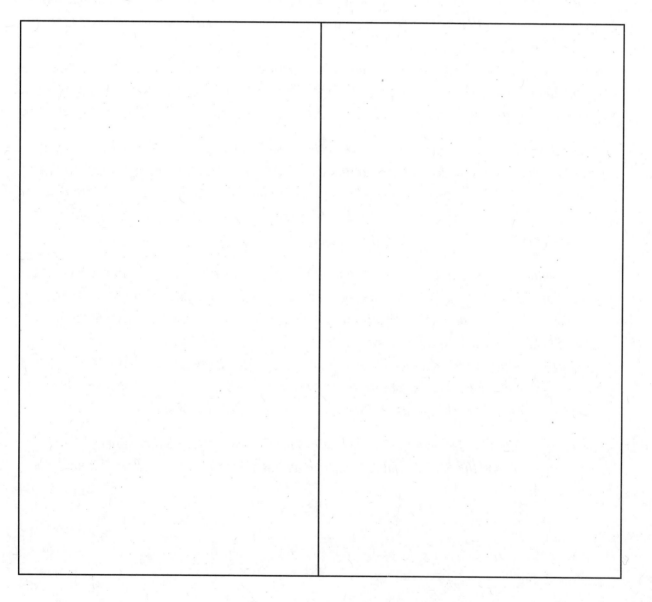

Can you think of a time when you were stuck in a threat-drive loop like Ella's? What did this feel like in your body, thoughts, and feelings? Did you feel balanced?

_____

_____

_____

_____

_____

Think of a challenging time when your threat circle dominated the other circles. How did that affect your confidence? Was there anything you did that made your threat circle bigger or smaller?

_____

_____

_____

_____

_____

In the coming weeks, notice when you are in threat, and just be curious. You might even tell yourself something like, *Oh, that's just my threat mind*. From there, you can try to use mindfulness or another skill to activate soothing—something we'll explore in the next activity and throughout this workbook.

more to do

You can actually learn to shift out of threat and into soothing. And the more you can do this, the more balanced your emotions, and the more you can respond to life's setbacks from a position of wisdom, strength, and helpful action.

Activating your soothing system will increase your confidence to deal with whatever life throws at you. One way to activate your green circle and quiet your red is to learn to regulate your breathing. This works because when you adjust your breathing, you change your body, your physiology, and your brain, which changes your mood, your focus, and your impulses. You have the power to shift from your sympathetic nervous system (red circle, or your threat response) to your parasympathetic nervous system (green circle, or your soothing system).

We offer some breathing basics to calm yourself and avoid getting hijacked by setbacks and emotions. Once you have some practice, try this as an anchor even in a confidence crisis.

Breath researchers tell us that the most beneficial rate and rhythm of breathing is about five or six full breath cycles per minute—that is, a breath cycle every ten or twelve seconds. It's also good to breathe out (exhale) for a bit longer than you breathe in (inhale).

Maybe you've noticed that when your breath is short or shallow, it usually means you are anxious and lacking in confidence. In fact, short shallow breaths are like dialing 911 and asking your brain and body to go into panic mode—not exactly where you'll feel your most confident. That's because different nerve endings in the top and bottom of the lungs send different signals to the nervous system for what to do.

Breathing in more deeply and more slowly is like hitting the reset button in your brain and body. It helps you calm yourself down and confidence yourself up. You can try different ways, but again, you want to aim for five or six full breaths a minute. When you find a slower, natural rhythm to your breathing, emotions settle down, your focus sharpens to let in more information, and you can you feel more at ease and interested socially.

It's been said, "Your breath is like a remote control: it can turn the volume on your anxiety or confidence up or down." Take some time to notice your breathing for ten breaths. Without changing anything, just breathe and count how many breath cycles you have in a minute, how long on the inhale, and how long on the exhale.

What numbers did you get?

3-6-9 Breathing: Now let's try changing the channel to 3-6-9 with your remote control. See what it's like to intentionally slow down your breathing rate using the 3-6-9 breath: breathing in as you count to three, holding your breath to six, and exhaling to nine. Try this for about ten breaths or until it feels comfortable.

Did you notice any changes in your mind or body?

What are some good times for shifting out of threat by using this breathing practice? Before a game? Before a test or public speaking? Social situations? Others?

Activating Your Green Circle

Slowing down your breathing is one way to activate your soothing system. Learning to speak to yourself less harshly, with less judgment, is another. Throughout this workbook you will learn lots more, including mindfulness and compassion practices to activate your soothing system and improve your confidence, especially when you need it the most. In the following green circle, review what you are willing to try to activate your soothing system and tap into a more confident state. As you go through this workbook and discover new ways to shift into your soothing system, we encourage you to return to this page and add to your list.

Check the boxes for things you are willing to try to activate your soothing system. Try to notice what helps you supercharge your green circle. Add to this list when you can, and note what works best for you.

MY GREEN CIRCLE

☐ Spend time with people I love.

☐ Snuggle with a pet.

☐ Remind myself: what I'm going through is hard.

☐ Take a rest in fresh air.

☐ Talk to a supportive friend who always makes me feel good.

☐ Reflect on blessings and past success.

☐ Tap into my inner ally's voice (Activity 4).

☐ Try a mindfulness exercise.

    ○ Mindful SEAT (Activity 8)

☐ Practice a confidence-boosting visualization

    ○ Merging with your inner ally (Activity 5)

    ○ Squad of Kindness (Activity 12)

    ○ Captain of the Ship (Activity 13)

☐ Give myself a pep talk.

☐ Listen to music that fills me up.

☐ Read books I find comforting.

☐ Ask myself what I need, and make time for it.

☐ Give myself a break and do something relaxing, like _____.

☐ Stretch gently into a confident posture (Activity 14).

☐ Take a self-compassion break (Activity 21).

☐ Try a guided meditation.

    ○ Just Like Me (Activity 8)

    ○ Taking and Sending (Activity 16)

☐ Try a breathing exercise.

    ○ 3-6-9 Breathing (Activity 2)

    ○ Sketch your breath (Activity 8)

_____

_____

_____

_____

avoidance and holding back 3

for you to know

In the last activity we discussed a setback or challenging situation that causes a stress response and triggers big emotions like anxiety or panic. Another common response to these kinds of situations is avoidance: the tendency to stay away from challenging situations.

Avoidance might seem to make things easier at first, but over time it worsens our struggle and holds us back from what we want. It can become a vicious downward spiral: Dealing with a setback can lower your self-confidence. Avoiding the situation that lowered your self-confidence can *reinforce* that low self-confidence, because you never learn whether you could actually do or get through whatever you're avoiding. A lack of self-confidence leads to more avoidance, which leads to more not practicing what you need to practice to get better, which leads to less skill and less self-confidence, and the problem snowballs as you feel worse and worse.

So, while it may feel better in the short term to avoid what you're not confident doing, it won't help you grow your confidence or cope with whatever you're avoiding. Like working out a muscle, you need to challenge yourself just enough.

On the flip side, if you can learn to *approach* what you might otherwise avoid—the situations that challenge you—often you'll find that you can actually get through them. You're often more capable than you think you are. And when you make the approach, your confidence in your own abilities and resilience—your ability to learn and grow from challenges—will increase. The key is being willing to act and to practice.

for you to do

Can you think of areas of your life where you might be on the sidelines? Read Mia's story, then answer the reflection questions and think about areas you might be avoiding.

Mia struggles with self-confidence in social situations. When she moved from her small elementary school to a much bigger middle school, everyone looked so confident. That intimidated Mia even more. She decided to just hang back and stay out of the way. She got in the habit of avoiding small talk and most interactions with other kids. And over time she got more out of practice talking to new people and making friends.

Eventually, Mia's parents had her see a therapist, who suggested that learning to be social is like learning the violin. "When you're learning the violin," she said, "the later you start, the more behind you can feel. But when you start later, you can also make progress faster because you're older." She encouraged Mia to just start practicing socializing like practicing her violin, without worrying so much about what would happen or thinking so hard about how intimidated she sometimes felt. "Try to be curious and open to whatever happens."

Mia found small steps she felt comfortable trying and building on. She started with simply paying more attention to her nonverbal communication with peers and making efforts to appear open to talking. She started smiling more and resisted her usual writing in her planner before class to avoid eye contact and small talk. Sure enough, she soon felt more comfortable, and she found herself responding when people started chatting. This led to starting more conversations, finding she had a lot in common with two girls, and eventually becoming friends with them. What helped her take small steps at the beginning was not focusing on the outcome. Instead of focusing on making friends on day one or the possible failure she might face, she reframed her efforts as practice that would help her feel more comfortable over time. She also found that taking even small steps at the beginning was empowering, as an alternative to doing nothing. As those small actions increased over time, Mia's confidence in talking to people and navigating social situations began to grow.

Did you relate to anything about Mia's story?

_____

_____

_____

What were some of the costs of her avoiding?

_____

_____

_____

What did she gain by avoiding? What helped her shift to action?

_____

_____

_____

When you avoid situations you don't feel confident in, what are the usual costs and benefits?

_____

_____

_____

What are the large and small places where you hold back? Socially with friends? At school? With sports, arts, and activities? In your family? Write a little about each.

_____

_____

_____

_____

_____

_____

_____

more to do

There are many situations that might be so stressful that we hold back. Our confidence falls, and our avoidance rises. We can't guarantee that when you finish this book you'll be making a prom-posal in costume in front of a stadium while sharing your SAT scores with everyone. But we can think about ways to get you moving toward your goals.

Look over the following list of situations where you might be playing it too safe and could use some confidence. Identify situations you want to move toward, ignoring items that don't relate to you and adding others that do. Rank the items you picked for how hard they seem, on a 1-to-10 scale and write them next to the ladder with the lower-ranked items at the bottom and higher-ranked items at the top. Then use the list as a reference for the situations and activities you might want to approach rather than avoid over time. Start with the easier situations, working your way up the ladder.

This can help you identify your goals, to start and continue at a reasonable pace, building on each success as you go along. Feel free to share this with a trusted friend or adult.

1	5	10
Easy as pie; I got this.	It would be hard but I can do it.	Nope. No way. Too hard right now.

Things I want to move toward

Driving alone (or with friends)

Public speaking

Walking into the cafeteria with no friends in sight

Going to a party by myself

Heading off to college with no one from my school with me

Meeting new people

Going to sleepaway camp or program

Wearing a new outfit to school

Inviting someone to the movies

Friending someone on social media

Job or college interviews

Going to therapy or counseling

Getting extra help after school

Asking someone on a date

Asking someone to hang out as a friend

Being around new people

Posting on social media

Going to a party

Trying out for a sports team, or auditioning for a play or musical group

Performing in front of a crowd: sports, music, theater, arts

Raising my hand in class

Being called on at random in class

Sending or responding to texts

Changing in the school locker room

Going to the gym or exercising

Eating in front of other people

Sitting at a new table in the cafeteria

Walking into the SAT or ACT

Sharing my writing or art with other people

Opening up to others about my feelings

Other situations _____

_____

With some of these, you may already be a few steps in or already feel confident. That's great. If not, that's fine too!

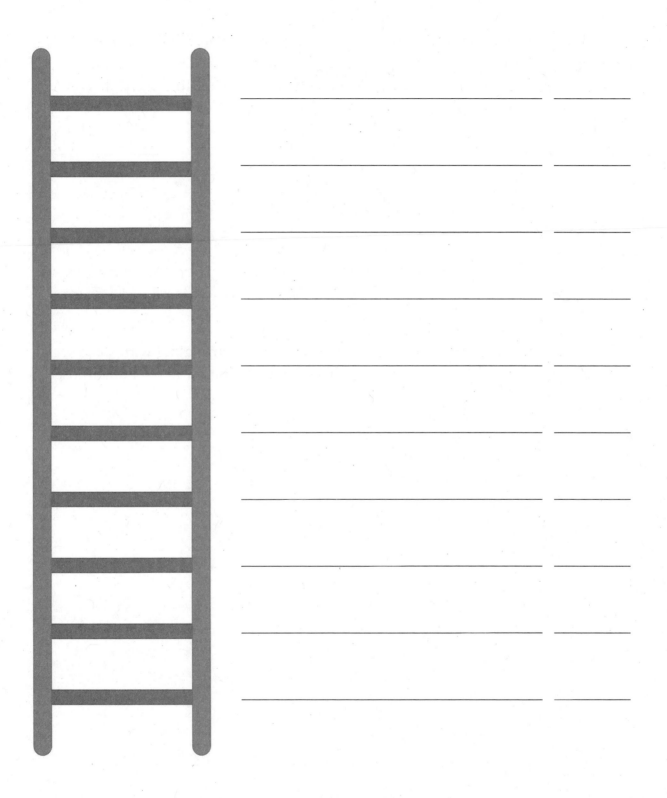

Now pick one item you haven't yet done and might want to do. What could help you move toward that first goal? Write a bit about how to get there. How could you break down your goal into small steps that could lead to bigger steps, like Mia did? When and how could you start?

_____

_____

_____

_____

_____

You might find, as you completed this activity, that you're struggling with some social fears. Check out Activity 15, Getting Out There, for more on how to deal with those.

for you to know

We've discussed two reactions to stress that not only block our confidence but make challenges worse as we get consumed by emotions and avoidance. Another unhelpful reaction is self-criticism. When you face a threat or challenge, it is common to harshly self-blame and self-criticize. That inner critic loves to jump in and kick you when you're down. That inner critic supercharges your threat mind, making it more difficult to self-soothe and bounce back. This can also cut into self-confidence, leaving you with more doubts and insecurity even after you calm down. So even though self-criticism is a go-to habit for many people, that inner bully just adds to your problems and messes up a healthy relationship with yourself.

If self-criticism is so bad for well-being and confidence, why do we do it? Unfortunately, our minds are designed not to keep us happy but to keep us safe. That inner critic is meant to protect us. The brain is programmed to trigger the well-known fight-or-flight response when we face something threatening. But these days humans face different dangers than we did when human brains first developed. We're confronting not snakes or saber-toothed tigers, but threats to our sense of self, including our confidence. Still, the old fight-or-flight stress response kicks in—and we attack ourselves.

Let's say you slip and fall in the hallway. You don't get injured, but when you're there on the floor with everyone staring at you, your ego takes a blow. You're already feeling hurt from the fall, and then the inner critic adds something like *Great job, idiot! You couldn't be more clumsy if you tried!* Often the inner critic is harsher than our peers! Now you feel ready to crawl into a hole, never to be seen again.

In this example, the fall in front of the other kids triggered your fight-or-flight response to stress. The critic, by name-calling, is trying to protect you and spare you from future humiliation. The problem is that doesn't really work. In fact, believing the critic makes things worse and drains self-confidence. Although this is frustrating, it's important to remember the inner critic is not an enemy we need to fight. It's helpful to think of the inner critic more like a young kid that is trying to "help" but does so in ways that aren't so helpful. In fact, when we have some understanding and compassion for our critic, we can deal with it more effectively. Let's look at some specific ways to work with your inner critic.

for you to do

You probably know some kids who try to get lots of attention on social media, maybe even go viral. You generally scroll past their posts, but sometimes you pay more attention than you should. This can happen when you take your inner critic's messages as fact. When you pay attention and believe what your inner critic says, that drowns out more helpful, wiser inner voices, leaving you feeling pretty bad about yourself.

Think about times when your inner critic is active. What do they say, and how do you react? Do you listen as if the message were fact, or can you see it as chatter and noise? To get to know your inner critic a bit more, answer the following questions:

My inner critic's favorite phrases and messages about me:

_____

_____

_____

_____

_____

My inner critic is the loudest when:

_____

_____

_____

_____

My inner critic is most scared by and trying to protect me from:

_____

_____

_____

_____

When I believe my inner critic and take the messages as fact, what happens?

_____

_____

_____

_____

How might I benefit from learning to observe my inner critic and hear their messages as noise?

_____

_____

_____

_____

more to do

Have you ever noticed how good it can feel to mute or hide people on your social media? Once you've unsubscribed or muted a given user, you've removed their influence over you and can focus on healthier voices. You can do the same with your inner critic.

Step 1: Label the Critic

To quiet the inner critic, step one is naming them. This alone can calm you down and mute their messages. Some people like the label "inner critic"; others use "the judge" or an innocent name to take them less seriously. Like, "Oh, that's just Lucy" or "There's Bob again." Draw your inner critic here to remind you they're not a powerful enemy, but more like the kid online trying to get your attention and get their post to go viral.

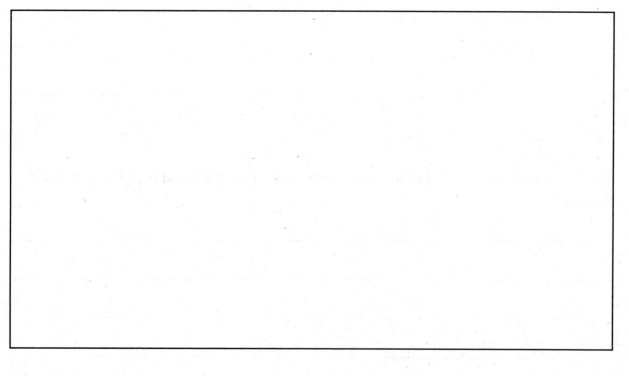

I name my critic: _____

Step 2: Step Back and Observe

Once you name your critic and know who you're dealing with, you can learn to step back and just watch. Rather than wrestling or arguing with the thoughts, you can just see them for what they are: an overprotective, ineffective stress response trying to keep you safe.

It helps to have some prepared responses that can help you step back and unsubscribe from your critic. Check the statements that resonate for you, and feel free to add your own.

- ☐ *There goes my inner critic. He is doing his thing.*

- ☐ *Hi there, inner critic. I see you feel like doing the blame game right now.*

- ☐ *Thanks, inner critic. I know you are trying to help. I know you're doing all you know how to do. But I got this today. I'm going to move on to other things that matter to me.*

- ☐ *What's up, little guy? I see you over there. I know you're trying to keep me safe and on top of things. You can rest if you like. You can stick around, too, but I have other things that need my attention.*

- ☐ *Hello, judge. I can make some space for you, but I am going to go back to what I was doing over here.*

- ☐ For any name calling, you can shift perspective from *I am stupid and awful* to a curious observation: *My inner critic thinks I'm stupid and awful. Interesting.* Perspective like this helps you not believe everything they say.

- ☐ _____

- ☐ _____

- ☐ _____

Note: Some people have extra loud critics that can make working with these skills a bit tricky. If you are someone who believes much of your critic's messaging, you might benefit from working with a therapist. If therapy isn't possible, consider discussing some of these ideas with a trusted adult.

Step 3: Bring Your Inner Ally Online

You also have another voice: an inner ally that can sometimes be hard to hear. Instead of blaming you, the inner ally is supportive and patient, like a loving friend or encouraging coach. Your inner ally has your back and your best interest at heart. They root for you when you win and comfort you when you face disappointment. They also offer constructive feedback and help you self-correct.

If you take time to develop a caring inner ally, you can access courage and wisdom to rebound from challenges. When you connect with your inner ally in difficult moments, you can see things differently. In fact, picturing your inner ally can activate your soothing system.

We want you to take a moment to imagine your inner ally. If you could imagine someone who is totally focused on caring for you, what would they look like, and what qualities would they have? Some of our clients choose a favorite fictional character with nurturing and compassionate qualities. Others choose real people who have been supportive, compassionate and kind. And some even imagine their inner ally as a wise and compassionate version of themselves.

As you imagine your inner ally, think about someone who sees how hard things can be for you, who understands and completely accepts you, and who really cares about you and wants to help you—the way you really care about and would want someone you really loved. Keep in mind this ally is there to help you cope, and has a strength where they don't get overwhelmed when things get tough. In addition, this ally is warm, kind, accepting, and wise. How would this person support and encourage you?

Now draw what your inner ally looks like, and list their best qualities.

I will call my inner ally: _____

My inner ally's qualities:

_____

_____

_____

When do I most need to connect with my inner ally?

_____

_____

_____

What might my inner ally tell me when I am upset, and how would they say it? (For more on how to manage when you mess up, check out Activity 21.)

_____

_____

_____

5 working with shame

for you to know: defining shame

There's another barrier to self-confidence: the emotion known as shame. It has a special relationship with the inner critic. Shame can be tricky to navigate because it has many faces and disguises, and it can hide beneath other emotions and behaviors. In fact, we don't always realize shame is taking over.

What is shame? It's a painful feeling telling you that you are somehow inferior and bad at your core; a feeling that "There is something wrong with me," or a sense that if someone really knew you, they'd find you unacceptable. Dr. Paul Gilbert (2022) identifies two types: external and internal. Look at these descriptions and think about times when you might have felt either one.

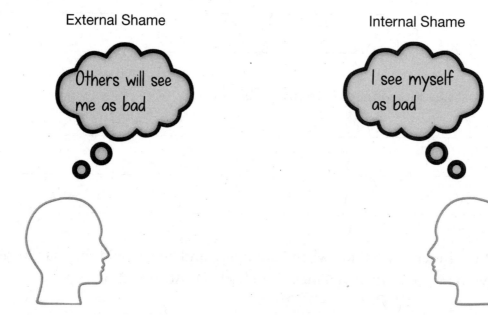

External Shame

Others will see me as bad

The fear or belief that others will find you unacceptable or bad in some way. Often linked to social anxiety.

Internal Shame

I see myself as bad

Belief that you are damaged, unworthy, or bad at the core, regardless of what others think. Mistakes are seen as proof of how flawed you are. Linked to depression and anxiety.

You might experience both forms of shame or one more than the other. Both are pretty unpleasant. But shame is a universal emotion, and even though it feels bad, it is essential to our survival. Think of shame not as some kind of villain but as a safety signal to keep you in check. It can kick in when you've behaved in ways others might not like—and can serve as a way to know when you should adjust your behavior. Of course, shame can also kick in unnecessarily or stick around too long. When shame lingers, it can take over, leading to a paralyzing downward spiral. If the inner critic piles on, shame gets worse. In fact, shame and the inner critic tend to feed on each other in a vicious cycle, leaving you feeling more stuck than ever.

Many people describe shame as a feeling like they are sinking in quicksand. We like that image, because it turns out quicksand won't actually suck you down like in the movies. It's actually almost impossible to drown in quicksand because it is twice as dense as the human body. If you got caught in quicksand, it would be unpleasant, but you would actually float, not drown. And just as the best way to get out of quicksand is to float to solid ground and wiggle out with slow, steady movements, when shame arises you can also move slowly to solid ground, emotionally, to find your way out of it, rather than struggling and feeling stuck.

for you to do

Both internal and external shame are barriers to self-confidence and connection with others. But as with quicksand, if we can learn to slow down rather than struggle, we can move through shame. Think about how this might relate to your experience:

Think of a time you experienced internal or external shame. What did each feel like? How did they impact your confidence?

_____

_____

_____

_____

Where do you feel shame in your body? If you're not sure, pay attention next time and return here to jot down any observations.

_____

_____

_____

_____

more to do

Shame is less scary when you remember it is just a safety signal from your brain warning you of disconnection. The inner critic is not going to help you when you feel shame; it will just make it worse. The antidote to shame is self-compassion, a core theme of this book and core part of our soothing system. There are many ways to develop self-compassion and activate your soothing system, such as tapping into your inner ally and staying curious rather than judgmental. Judging yourself just deepens the quicksand of shame and the threat system.

A good start to staying curious and disrupting the shame/inner critic cycle is to first simply name them. This can help you avoid feeling sucked in deeper. Remember, they are not your enemies, but an overprotective response to setbacks. It can also be helpful to name where you feel shame in your body, to get a little distance from your thoughts. Check the comments you can use to name and observe the quicksand from solid ground, without sinking into it. Feel free to add your own statements.

☐ *This is shame. It is just an emotion that is normal and part of the human experience.*

☐ *Hi, shame. And hello, inner critic jumping into the mix.*

☐ *This is just my threat mind.*

☐ *This is simply a safety signal from my mind working hard to try to protect me.*

☐ *Shame and the inner critic are visiting. Let me tap into my inner ally. I know I need my compassionate voice when I'm in threat.*

☐ _____

☐ _____

☐ _____

Your inner ally from the last activity can help you disrupt shame by moving you out of threat and into courage, strength, and wisdom to navigate whatever situations you might face. Calling up your inner ally can be a powerful way to keep the shame at bay. The following meditation can help you tap in to your inner ally. (An audio version is available as a free tool at http://www.newharbinger.com/50492.)

Meditation: Merging with Your Inner Ally

Use this practice to strengthen your inner ally and more effectively work with shame and your inner critic.

To begin, find a quiet spot where you won't be disturbed. In a comfortable, upright position, slowly begin to focus on your breath. Slow down and simply notice your inhale and exhale. Now find a breathing rhythm that is just right for you—maybe counting to four on the in-breath and again on the out-breath.

When your mind wanders, remember that this is normal, and simply bring your attention back to your breathing and start again. Think of an excited puppy: You understand that is their nature, so you don't judge them. Puppies can be too hyper, but they don't mean any harm. They often just need some guidance. Can you have that attitude toward your mind? If it wanders, gently bring yourself back by saying *puppy mind* or *thinking*.

After a few minutes of focusing on your breathing, narrow your attention to the area around your heart. Place one hand on your heart as you continue to breathe and notice your chest area.

Then, still connected to your breathing and your chest, bring to mind the image of your inner ally. This can be a fictional character, a real-life person, a collective of nurturing individuals, or even yourself in your most compassionate and wise form. This inner ally is full of wisdom and courage and is deeply committed to your well-being. Sense their powerful, caring, nonjudging presence.

Now imagine a beam of light connecting your heart to the heart of your inner ally. Feel yourself taking in their positive qualities of compassion, wisdom, nonjudgment, and confidence.

Imagine the light connecting your hearts growing more intense as you take in their strengths. Imagine the distance between your hearts disappearing, as the light pulls you closer to their heart. Imagine the light pulls you so close that you have merged with your inner ally and are now one. Continue to sit quietly as you imagine taking in your inner ally's qualities, allowing their kindness and strength to travel from your heart throughout your body.

As you end the meditation, open your eyes and remember that your inner ally is always there inside you, available when you need them. You can always bring them with you throughout the day, no matter who or what you meet along the way.

After trying this practice, how do you feel? What does your body feel like? Do you notice any changes in your heart, body, or mind?

_____

_____

_____

Did you find your mind wandering during the practice? Were you able to gently bring your attention back without being critical or harsh with yourself, just like training a cute puppy?

_____

_____

When might this practice be helpful for you? Can you think of scenarios where it might be helpful to merge with your ally?

_____

_____

Conclusion

We hope that this first section helped you understand self-confidence and why it's a struggle for so many of us. We saw how we can get swept up in threat (red circle) after setbacks. Then we explored ways to activate the soothing circle (green). We also looked at avoidance, the inner critic, and how to work with shame. With the help of mindfulness and compassion, we will build on these core areas throughout the book to enhance your confidence and resilience. In the next section, we will start to explore more specific actions you can take to boost your confidence throughout your day. The remaining activities will relate to the blocks in part 1, with more on how to shift out of threat (red circle) and into a more helpful, confident, and centered state of being (green circle). Feel free to come back to this section at any time.

Which aspects of part 1 were most helpful to you?

_____

_____

_____

_____

PART 2

School Days

In this section, we'll start to look at school, a place where many of us struggle with confidence. There are so many reasons school days can be a trigger, from the awkwardness of being early or late to class, to raising your hand or talking with teachers, to those class presentations that just about everyone seems to dread.

There may be other things that make school a challenge for you. Maybe you are the new kid, or you've had some tough social experiences in the past. Maybe you've had some bad experiences in classes, with less-than-understanding teachers. You may have your own learning differences that prevent you from feeling entirely comfortable and confident in the school building. Or sometimes factors related to culture, gender, or sexual identity can play a role.

What are some underlying issues that might also undermine your confidence at school? Do any of the blocks in the previous section—setbacks, avoidance, the inner critic, or shame—play a role in your confidence at school?

Whatever might limit your confidence at school, know that the skills you'll learn in the activities in this section can apply. Though this is designated the school section, you can still use these exercises in all kinds of settings. The work you do to build your confidence, and your willingness to approach the things that make you nervous rather than avoid them, will help you even after your school days are far behind you.

6 getting centered before school

for you to know

Some of us wake up fresh and ready to start the day with confidence. Others wake up with a sense of dread about the day ahead, already feeling deflated and defeated before the day has even begun.

But your morning routine can be a place where you bring a bit more *mindfulness* to boost your confidence and keep self-doubt at bay. Mindfulness is a way of observing your own experience with curiosity and without judgment. It's also a good skill to have as you continue to approach the things that low self-confidence might prefer that you avoid.

Rather than starting your day by going through the motions with little thought, there are many ways you can use the principles of mindfulness and intention to try to stay balanced to get the day off to a good start. Try building some of these into your routine, and see if things shift a bit as you prep for school.

for you to do

Look through the following rituals and think about which ones might help you feel centered.

- **Get moving**: When you wake up in the morning, try a little mindful movement. Maybe just some gentle stretches or sun salutations from yoga. Find a short, easy exercise video online that can help you feel confident and capable for whatever the day brings.

- **Clean and fresh**: Regular hygiene routines offer great spots to practice getting centered using your senses. When you shower, instead of getting lost in thought, make an effort to feel the sensations of the warm water on your skin, smell the soap, hear the sounds, taste and see the steam in the air. Try to use brushing your hair or teeth, putting on makeup, or any other morning preparations to notice sensations rather than doing them on autopilot.

- **Dress for success**: Choose clothes that make you feel confident, the outfits that help you feel like you're capable. Many people find dressing a certain way can boost their confidence going into the day.

- **Walk with purpose**: Some people find that when they hold their head up high and keep their posture confident, it's easier for them to let criticism from others or self-criticism roll off right off. Make an effort to stand tall, relax your shoulders, and see if you don't stay a bit boosted as your day goes on.

- **Musical motivation**: Have you got your own pump-it-up soundtrack? Make yourself a playlist that gets you motivated and enthusiastic. You can get yourself dancing and move your body for a bit, if that helps, or stay still and just listen— say, on your ride to school.

After reading through these ideas, what ritual could you try to help you intentionally start your day more grounded? What could be the benefit of starting your day with intention rather than rushing frantically or going through the motions of your morning tasks? How might a centering ritual or intention at the start of your day influence your attitude and confidence?

_____

_____

_____

_____

_____

_____

for you to know

You might wake up already worried about school, or overcome with self-doubt. Often when your mind brings your attention to the negative like this, there is a good reason. There's an important problem that your brain may be able to solve.

However, worries are often related to the brain's negativity bias. In the words of our dear friend Dr. Rick Hanson, the negatives of life stick to our brain like Velcro, while the positives tend to naturally bounce off.

This negativity bias is why the brain often keeps streaming the self-doubt show on repeat, all day and all night. But we can't always think our way out of every problem; we've got more important things to do! That's when the worrying brain becomes more useless than useful.

If your brain's negativity bias is driving many of your self-doubts, here's a silly-sounding exercise that just might help. Worry on purpose! Many psychologists who have studied worry find that this can be really helpful. It reminds us of the following story.

> Once upon a time, there was a man who wanted to practice meditation. But every time he sat down to meditate, he was plagued with worries and doubt. The more he struggled with his worries, the more they grew, leaving him so frustrated that he would simply give up.

(Sound familiar?)

> Finally he decided to consult the meditation master on the mountaintop. The guru's advice was simple: "This time, I want you to take your meditation posture, set your timer for five minutes, and just worry—nothing else."

> The man went back down the mountain, blew the dust off his meditation cushion, set a timer, and began to worry. But he found that no matter how hard he tried to worry, after

just a few minutes his mind would wander. The worries wouldn't stick around. So he headed back up the mountain to complain to the guru.

"Well," said the master, "the mind is a funny thing. Now try starting with your worries, and then try meditating again."

The man returned home, this time to find that when he purposely began with a bit of worrying, he was able to settle more easily into his meditation practice.

This story shows us that if we invest time and energy to struggling with worries, they can grow. But if we can learn to flip what some call the "struggle switch"—to be with our worries without trying to make them go away—the worries tend to move on more easily. We can even take advantage of the mind's tendency to wander. As the man learned, if we *lean* into the worries without struggle, they sometimes run their course and wander off.

With that, we invite you to worry on purpose, so that your worries can actually move on.

for you to do

Whether it's the worries that come in the morning or the ones that find you throughout the day, you can try to worry on purpose.

Begin by finding a comfortable place and posture to sit and let yourself worry. Set a timer for maybe five minutes, and begin with a small worry or contemplate a situation where you lack confidence. Notice where and how the worry and doubt appear in your body, or how long those sensations last. At the end of your five minutes, the time to deliberately focus on your worry is over—at least for now. Purposely return to whatever is next on your schedule. If and when the worries try to sneak back in, allow them to stay in the background while you focus on what's in front of you here and now.

After purposefully worrying, answer these questions:

What happened to your worry? Did your mind wander off? Did the worries fade?

_____

_____

_____

At the end of the day, think back:

What about the rest of your day? Did your session of worrying on purpose make worry easier to deal with afterward?

_____

_____

_____

The man in the story felt more settled when he turned off his struggle switch and stopped trying to make his worries go away. How might you turn off your struggle switch when you worry? How could shifting the way you approach those morning worries affect your confidence and the rest of your day?

_____

_____

_____

_____

confidence in the classroom 8

for you to know

Have you ever been the first one to class or on campus? You might feel like kind of a loser for being early, or awkward when it's just you and the teacher and then the teacher's pets come in. Or maybe you've felt the embarrassment of being the last kid to come to class, feeling everyone's eyes on you as you slink to your seat. And so many things in between can lead to a confidence crunch in the classroom.

Do these situations make you want to avoid, withdraw, or hide? It might help to recognize what triggers this. Being the first to class? Being last? Some other circumstance that puts you in the spotlight?

Maybe there are things that set you off into worry spirals during class. What do you typically worry about then: what other kids are thinking and doing, what the teacher thinks about you, whether you'll get called on, the work in class, a pop quiz?

for you to do

Jane's confidence crashed whenever she got to class, even after a great lunch or a walk in the hallway with friends. Her thoughts raced and her heart pounded. To calm herself down, she'd developed a whole routine for class: She used 3-6-9 breathing, putting a hand on her heart, and other mindfulness practices.

She also found it helpful at the start of every class to follow the Mindful SEAT, a practice you can do at any time. (An audio version is available as a free tool at http://www.newharbinger.com/50492.)

Briefly check in with yourself about your

- **S**enses and sensations

- **E**motions

- **A**ctions

- **T**houghts

To begin, imagine yourself walking into class and sitting down. Then reflect on the following:

S: Senses and Sensations

What are your senses telling you right now?

What do you *see* that gives you information about safety, danger, or something else?

What do you *hear* that tells you anything about safety, danger, or something else?

What do you *taste* or *smell*?

More deeply, what sensations do you feel in your body? Is your body hot or cool? Is your heart rate fast or slow? What other signals is your body sending you right now? Do they reflect reality?

_____

_____

_____

_____

_____

E: Emotions

What emotions do you feel right now? Are you confident or anxious? Happy or sad? Peaceful or angry? Frustrated? Worried? Bored? Calm or agitated? Are these emotions accurate or helpful in this moment?

_____

_____

_____

_____

_____

A: Actions

What actions do you feel like taking, or what urges or impulses do you feel? Do you want to make a nasty comment? Flee from the room, screaming? Just say "Forget it" and put your head down on your desk? Or are you motivated to attend class and do what you need to do to be a good friend to yourself in this moment? What actions could be more helpful in this moment?

_____

_____

_____

_____

_____

T: Thoughts

What thoughts are coming up? Maybe dire thoughts like these: *I'm gonna fail! I hate this teacher! This class is so boring. I hope Ben doesn't sit next to me.*

_____

_____

_____

_____

_____

more to do

Now reflect on your SEAT experience and answer the following questions:

Was the information you got from this this mindful check-in an accurate reflection of reality? Was it helpful or not so helpful when it comes to feeling more confident in yourself and what you're doing?

_____

_____

_____

The next time you're in a similar situation, what could you do to befriend your experience so you can better manage any self-doubt that arises?

_____

_____

_____

Think of some other times you could use the Mindful SEAT; for instance, meetings or extracurricular activities:

_____

_____

Over the next week or so, try using the Mindful SEAT practice in your daily life. Just run through the letters in your mind as you focus on your own experience. See if the practice helps you understand more precisely what you're feeling as you face a challenge. And see if any action helps you recover some of the self-confidence and security you need.

9 speaking up in class

for you to know

You're seated and settled into class, but sometimes that's only half the battle. You may still struggle with confidence in particular moments—say, when you're about to raise your hand and speak up, or when the teacher calls on you. Maybe your mind freezes up as soon as you are called on, or races with fears about saying something embarrassing or stupid.

This is your mind reacting to what feels like a threat: being put on the spot in front of your teachers and classmates. It's an understandable response, but not one that's likely to help you in the situation, since the threat your body's reacting to isn't the kind of thing you can fight against or run from.

When you're being called upon to perform in some way, and anxiety leaves you feeling shaky and unconfident, it's a great opportunity to again try out that handy remote control, your breath.

for you to do

Earlier in this book, you learned how your breath pattern corresponds to your moods and emotions, and how your mood corresponds to your breath pattern. Try sketching a few waves like this, representing your breath in the moments when you're calm and normal—absorbed in doing something you enjoy, or maybe not doing much of anything.

Then sketch your breath when you feel anxious. It might look something like this:

Now sketch your anxious breath, gradually calming and growing confident:

Now sketch a calm, confident breath:

The next time you feel anxious, in class or anywhere, try sketching your breath. Depict it as it flows while you're feeling anxious, then as you adjust your breathing to see what happens. You can also try to identify your ideal breathing for any scenarios where you might need a bit more confidence, doodle the pattern for it here or in a separate notebook or journal, and trace the line as you breathe—say, while you're in class, without anyone else even noticing.

more to do

After you have sketched your breathing, answer these questions.

Did you notice any different patterns to your breathing when you are more emotional? What were they?

_____

_____

_____

_____

What patterns do you notice when you are feeling calmer and more confident?

_____

_____

_____

_____

_____

10 assertiveness

for you to know

You may also feel less than confident when asserting yourself with teachers or authority figures. We get it; this can be hard and uncomfortable. However, asserting yourself calmly is an important life skill that can enhance your confidence and help you better manage stress.

Being assertive means speaking up for yourself without disrespecting anyone else. It's a communication skill that's essential to your confidence and healthy relationships, and one you can practice and improve on. Building assertiveness usually requires two things: practicing healthy communication skills while respecting yourself and the listener. This means learning how to mindfully speak up rather than staying silent, but without talking down to or attacking your audience. When you can deliver your message with respect, people tend to be less defensive and listen better. This is key to more productive conversations and stronger relationships.

The more you practice assertiveness, the easier it gets. The following story shows four different communication styles and how you can enhance yours.

Mrs. Meyers was a no-nonsense teacher known for being firm with her students. They liked her but were also a little scared of her. When taking an exam, her students noticed that the last few questions didn't make sense. Most of them were too scared to say a word.

All but two students were avoidant *communicators. But Jay wasn't one of them. He decided to confront Mrs. Meyers. He launched into the conversation pretty strongly, using "you" statements that felt like accusations. He began, "You made an unfair exam," and the conversation went downhill from there. Although Jay was confident enough to speak up, he used an* aggressive *style that didn't respect his teacher. Jay didn't take the time to think through how he was coming across and Mrs. Meyers was so put off that Jay's point was lost.*

Natalia decided to send an email. She didn't want to upset Mrs. Myers the way Jay had. But her email was vague and indirect. Not understanding what Natalia was trying to say, Mrs. Meyers politely replied with textbook page numbers for further reading. Natalia's email was respectful but used a passive, indirect communication style. So, like Jay, she didn't get her message across.

Natalia realized that she was being indirect out of a lack of confidence. Mrs. Meyers couldn't read her mind. So Natalia decided to change her approach and try again. She reminded herself it was normal to be nervous about speaking to a teacher. She also decided to connect with her motivation—why she needed to speak up in the first place. She reminded herself that she was approaching Mrs. Meyers both to clarify her confusion, to practice assertiveness skills (something she knew could use extra practice with), and to possibly get a better grade. Natalia took some time to intentionally come up with a direct, clear question she could ask the next day.

On her second try, Natalia was assertive. She used "I" statements with Mrs. Meyers—statements that made her own feelings and opinions clear, without being accusatory toward Mrs. Meyers.

"I think I found possible mistakes in the last two questions of the exam," she said, then made a respectful, direct request: "Would you be willing to double check and give credit if there are any errors?"

Mrs. Meyers was able to see that Natalia was right. She gave Natalia credit and appreciated her kindness and confidence. She also let the rest of the students in the class know she would double-check the exam questions and give credit where it was due. Natalia realized that her teacher wasn't that scary after all, and they went on to have a stronger relationship. Mrs. Meyers was a person with feelings and challenges, just like Natalia.

for you to do

Considering the different communication styles in Natalia's story—avoidant, indirect, aggressive, and assertive—think about your typical communication style and answer the following questions.

Do you have a typical communication strategy when it comes to friends, teachers, or meeting new people? Are you more assertive in some areas and more passive in others? In which areas could you benefit from speaking up with more assertiveness?

_____

_____

_____

How do you think using "I" statements focused on yourself, rather than "you" statements focused on the listener, affects communication?

_____

_____

_____

What steps might you take to speak up for yourself in challenging areas? Would you consider easier situations to start—maybe speaking up at stores and restaurants?

_____

_____

_____

more to do

Natalia's story shows how using an assertive communication style helped her see that Mrs. Meyers was not as intimidating as she and her classmates had assumed. A short mindfulness practice called Just Like Me can be useful before you speak up. The practice can help you remember what we all share, rather than getting tripped up on differences. (An audio version is available as a free tool at http://www.newharbinger .com/50492.)

Start by identifying someone to think about. It could be someone you would like to speak up to, like a teacher or a coach, or a more neutral person, like the restaurant server bringing your dinner. Even if you have many differences with this person, there are likely many ways the person is just like you. Bring the person to mind and remind yourself:

This person

- Has a body and a mind, just like me.

- Has feelings and thoughts, just like me.

- Has stress, just like me.

- Has been nervous, just like me.

- Has had setbacks, just like me.

- Has worries, just like me.

- Has challenges with others, just like me.

- Is learning about life, just like me.

- Wishes to be happy, just like me.

Now allow wishes of health and happiness for this person to arise. Say,

"I wish this person to be peaceful and happy."

"I wish this person to be loved because this person is a human being, just like me."

What was this practice like for you? When might it be helpful to use Just Like Me in your life?

_____

_____

_____

_____

_____

_____

for you to know

At the beginning of this workbook you read about Ella, who was having a hard time recovering from her low SATs. In activity 2, we looked at how she learned to activate her soothing system so she wasn't so overwhelmed. A few other things also helped her through confidence crunches at school.

Ella discovered that she had the wrong idea about intelligence. Ella entered therapy thinking either people are smart or they are not. And after her first disastrous practice SAT score, she was thinking she might not be that smart. This impacted not only her confidence, but also her efforts to study. If she was convinced that she wasn't that smart, what would be the point of studying, anyway?

Ella's therapist challenged her to rethink her view of intelligence, achievement, and failures. Ella learned about the work of Carol Dweck, a Stanford researcher who has studied failure and success for decades.

Dr. Dweck (2007) identified two common mindsets: fixed and growth.

Fixed Mindset	Growth Mindset
• I'm either smart or dumb.	• I can get smarter with time and effort.
• If it's challenging, I should give up.	• I take on challenges and learn from them.
• Effort is pointless.	• Effort pays off.
• Feedback is not welcomed.	• Feedback helps me learn.
• Others' success makes me feel bad.	• Others' success inspires me.

Underachievement
Perform Below Potential

High Achievement
Perform to Full Potential

Dr. Dweck found that people with a growth mindset bounce back from failures and see setbacks as opportunities to learn and grow. She also learned that people with a fixed mindset see failure as inevitable, which leads them to give up and lose even more confidence.

But Dr. Dweck also discovered that people can change their mindsets. So if you have a more fixed mindset, you can learn to shift to a growth mindset, which helps you bounce back with confidence any time you feel disappointed.

The key is a flexible brain. When you learn something new or put effort into a new skill, hobby, or subject, you are actually changing your brain and making yourself smarter. The fancy term for this is *neuroplasticity*, which means that your actions have the power to change your brain. We get so many messages that we are just "smart" or "dumb." Neuroplasticity means that if you are struggling with a new skill or an academic subject, you can do something to actually get smarter or improve your skill.

Ella started to catch herself in a fixed mindset. She discovered this wasn't happening just with the SAT; she tended to apply this fixed mindset to anything that didn't come easily. She started noticing her fixed mindset and shifting to a more flexible mindset. One method was adding the powerful word "yet." Instead of saying "I am horrible at standardized tests," she shifted to "I didn't get the score I wanted *yet*." Over time Ella was able to have more of a growth mindset, helpful for times when she hit a wall in her academics or didn't achieve a goal.

for you to do

After learning about growth and fixed mindsets, reflect on how your mindset might be affecting your life.

What do you think about intelligence and abilities? Would you say you have more of a growth or a fixed mindset? What areas of your life could use more of a growth mindset?

_____

_____

_____

_____

When you're dealing with a setback, how might you benefit from a growth mindset versus a fixed mindset? How could that affect your confidence and your effort?

_____

_____

_____

_____

Where else might you have a fixed mindset? How could you reframe your views to more of a growth mindset? We have listed some examples to help you get started. Add in some examples from your life for how you can start purposely noticing and shifting from a fixed to a growth mindset.

Fixed	→	Growth
I can't do it.	→	I'm working on that. I'm still trying.
I'm terrible at geometry.	→	What can I do to get better?
I'm bad at studying.	→	I'm not great at that yet.
Everyone is better at soccer than I am.	→	I can find ways to practice and get better. What can I learn from others?
This is too hard.	→	I'm still trying, and with more practice, it will get easier.
	→	
	→	
	→	
	→	

the class presentation

for you to know

In this activity, we'll look at a task that stresses many of us out: public speaking, like when you're called on to give a presentation in class. Speaking as adults who organize conferences and do a lot of public speaking, we can tell you that many people have confidence struggles with public speaking. So the secret of public speaking isn't trying to not be scared. The secret is to be scared—which is natural—and just do it anyway.

Often the hardest part of public speaking is not even the part when you're speaking. It's the minute or two right before you have to do it. If you can get through that time, it's usually fine.

And there are strategies you can use when you start to feel nervous. A friend who was an actor for many years taught me a little trick that I still use to this day: he calls it "flip the fear." The idea is to notice your body's fear reactions emerging from your doubt, but rather than letting them make you feel panicked, you tell yourself that you are actually excited.

Imagine being on a roller coaster: the cars are slowly chugging up a steep slope, and your heart starts to pound, your breath gets short, your palms start sweating. The car goes over the top and down, picking up speed. Now you are screaming, but you're having fun!

"Flip the fear" works on the same principle. Even if you can only partly convince yourself that what you're feeling just before doing something nerve-racking is excitement, not fear, it can make a real difference in terms of confidence.

for you to do

Think about how you might use flipping the fear in your life, then answer the following questions.

What are some situations, at school or elsewhere in life, where you get nervous because you're in public, or attracting attention in some way? It could be public speaking, or activities like sports, or social situations like dating.

_____

_____

_____

_____

What are some ways your body tells you it's either nervous or excited in these moments (heart pounding, breath speeding up, and so on)?

_____

_____

_____

_____

Now try visualizing yourself in one of those situations but instead thinking that it's actually not fear you're feeling, but excitement.

Or maybe it feels better—and more honest—to think that it's actually both fear *and* excitement you're feeling, but you don't have to let the fear dominate.

Next time you have to do a presentation, in class or anywhere, see if you can flip the fear. Can you convince yourself that you're not just scared but also excited? Maybe you're excited to share your work with the class, even as you're a little nervous about presenting it. After all, if you did good work on the presentation, odds are it's worth having confidence in your work! Or maybe you can feel how excited you are to try out for the team and show off your skills, even if you're a little nervous about it too. Or how excited you are to audition for the play, even though you're a little apprehensive about it.

Whatever the situation, if you can find ways to flip your fear—to interpret the sensations of nervousness as signs of excitement too—chances are it'll boost your confidence.

more to do

The poet Maya Angelou once shared some secrets of confidence. Before public speaking, she would imagine bringing with her everyone who had ever been kind to her. She would say, "Come with me. I need you now." This gave her an added dose of support and reinforcement, which likely helped her confidence and performance. She considered the helpers in her life as rainbows in her clouds, and she aimed to be a rainbow in other people's clouds. (Search "Maya Angelou, rainbow in the clouds" to find many short videos.)

Who have been the rainbows in your clouds? If you could create an imaginary squad of kindness to take with you before you speak, who would make your squad?

_____

_____

_____

What situations in your life could benefit from a kindness squad, and how could that help your performance?

_____

_____

_____

As you go through your day, consider how you could be part of a kindness squad for other people in your life—increasing the confidence and kindness in the world around you.

performing under pressure 13

for you to know

The class presentation is one of the many hoops you will jump through in high school. But what about the hoops that can feel a little more "do or die"? Whether you are up to bat in the championship game, going on a college interview, or about to sit for your last ACT, high school comes with some high stakes and waves of pressure. This is when self-confidence can give you the boost you need.

However, when you feel there's a lot riding on the results, it can feel like your confidence and guts are out of reach. The author Ernest Hemingway defined "guts" as having grace under pressure. Even if you are shy or feel you don't naturally have lots of guts just yet, you can learn to shift into a more centered state in those pressure-cooker moments. A practice called Multiple Selves, created by Dr. Paul Gilbert, can help build your confidence under pressure, even when you have more butterflies than you care to admit.

The following story (adapted with permission from Kolts, 2016, and Kolts & Chodron, 2015) introduces the idea of having multiple selves. (An audio version is available as a free tool at http://www.newharbinger.com/50492.)

Captain of the Ship

Imagine a ship sailing in the ocean with a mix of passengers. Each passenger is a version of you, representing a different feeling state. There's "angry you," "sad you," "anxious you," and any other emotional state.

Now imagine what these different versions of you would be doing. What might the angry you be doing as you sail the calm waters? Perhaps the anxious you is on the lookout deck with binoculars, scouting all the horrible things they predict will happen.

Imagine what happens as you pass through an inevitable storm. As the storm intensifies, the passengers get emotional in their own unique way. What does angry you do as the storm intensifies? Are they raging, screaming, and blaming anyone in their path? Perhaps anxious you is hiding or pacing somewhere, as they are certain this is the end! What about the sad, giving up version of you?

The good news is that the angry, anxious, and sad versions of you do not take the wheel of the ship. This ship has a captain, made for moments like this. The captain understands rough seas and knows what needs to be done. They not only navigate the ship with expertise but also stay calm and centered in the eye of the storm. Best of all, the captain is actually another version of you: the confident you, the one that is wise and has the courage to lead the ship to safety.

The captain is so steady that they also tame the chaos of the ship by calming the passengers. They are not annoyed by anger's yelling nor distracted by anxiety's panic. They understand that none of the passengers are bad and none of them need to go overboard. They just need reassurance. To the captain, what they're doing makes sense, because each is just doing what they know to do in a scary storm. And from this understanding place, the captain comforts each with their presence and words.

The confident captain is full of compassion, which gives them the strength to handle the pressure and comfort the passengers. The captain leads the way, with guts and grace. And each passenger feels safe with the captain at the helm. The captain knows exactly how to get all of them to safety. The captain is ready to rise to the challenge of this storm and any that follow.

The storm in this story is similar to the challenging storms of life, which include high-stakes, high-pressure scenarios that will come and go. The captain represents a state we can shift into to navigate challenges and the emotions that get loud in the storms. They remind us to be understanding rather than judging threat emotions or letting them take over and steer. Remember, you have multiple versions of yourself, including a calming, wise captain of your emotional life. Answer the following questions and reflect on how you might benefit from learning to shift into the wisest, bravest version of you, especially in times when a lot is on the line.

for you to do

Think of areas of your life where you are struggling with high pressure to perform. This could be game day, test taking, or trying to be more social in a noisy cafeteria.

_____

_____

_____

Close your eyes and try to think about a specific time when the anxious version of you took over during high pressure. What did it feel like in your body? What were your thoughts and feelings?

_____

_____

_____

How could learning to shift into a wise and confident version be helpful?

_____

_____

_____

In the next section of this activity, you'll connect with the confident captain inside you.

more to do

Find a comfortable place to read the following passage, reflect, and connect with the captain of your ship.

Sit comfortably and take a few minutes to slow down your inhale and exhale to a comfortable rhythm, slower than your normal breathing, almost like waves on the ocean.

Now close your eyes and invite the captain of your ship to the front of your mind. Bring to mind a confident version of you, courageous and wise. This captain starts with slowing things down. The slower inhale and exhale invites in a calm, steady presence. This presence is one that can help you navigate tricky waters with skill, wisdom, and courage.

As you imagine the captain taking over, you can feel courage that can help you perform at your best and a wisdom that keeps you focused on what matters. This confident version of you doesn't get overly focused on results or how you should measure up. Instead, it lets you be your best, meeting the moment with strength and resilience.

Continue to feel the qualities of your captain rising in you. This version of you was made to handle with grace whatever life might throw at you. This captain is here to help you rise to challenges—even in those high-pressure moments. This version of you is also understanding and nonjudgmental of you and all those emotions that may be swirling inside. This confident you understands what you want and is there to help you get where you want to go.

Your confident captain also understands that life is an epic journey that is more important than one result. The captain aims high but also knows that trying your very best is more important than outcomes. In fact, this confident you helps you filter out the noise and distractions of the pressure and keeps you focused on what is within your control. The confident version of you helps you find the right amount of effort, with faith you can handle whatever results. And if the outcome is disappointing, the confident version understands that this is part of the learning and part of your path. This confident you knows how to comfort and reassure you that nothing you go through is the last word about who or what you are. It knows that who you are is always changing, and that you can go through life with confidence, even when the path feels more like a storm.

As you imagine the confident, wise captain of your ship, take a few minutes to allow yourself to feel this state of being, with qualities of confidence, wisdom, and courage arising within you. Allow yourself to feel the strength and self-compassion rising like the tide. Your compassion for yourself fuels your strength to handle challenges rather than running away or letting emotions get the best of you. This version of you is willing to take risks with wisdom and effectiveness.

Feel this calm, centered state of the confident version of you, the version anchored in what matters, maintaining a steady heart in the midst of it all. With these qualities in your body, heart, and mind, take a few more breaths, breathing in the confidence and strength and allowing it to wash over you.

Then, when you are ready, reflect on the following questions.

What was it like to connect with the confident version of you? What did you notice in your body, thoughts, and feelings? And how did this differ from the anxious version of you responding to the first set of questions in "For You to Do"?

_____

_____

_____

_____

_____

What are some other times in your life when it'd be helpful to tap into the confident version of you?

_____

_____

_____

_____

_____

Even when the confident version of you tries to help, the result may not be what you wanted. How would your confident version handle the disappointment? What perspective would that wise version bring if you had to face a loss or disappointing outcome?

_____

_____

_____

_____

_____

for you to know

Growing up inevitably involves trying new things. School presents many new situations that can shake your confidence. Walking into a homeroom on the first day, going to the first meeting of a club you've just joined, trying a new sport, auditions, and more. What's worse, you may assume that everyone else is perfectly confident, so you get lost in all kinds of fears and worries that add to your doubts and shrink your confidence. But feeling unsure and not so confident when trying something new is a universal part of the human experience. Dr. Kelly Wilson humorously refers to these type of self-doubts as "human being growth syndrome." This always helps us remember not to make uncomfortable feelings into more than what they really are— normal feelings and sensations that arise when we are growing, trying, and learning.

We also encourage you to get out of your head and into a confident body. When you notice what's going on in your body, you can avoid getting trapped in overthinking, which is not helpful. Most of us naturally hold our bodies in certain ways when we are unsure. So another way to cultivate confidence is to find some confident postures you can tap into before you try something new, rather than unconsciously going with postures and gestures that signal doubt and fear.

It's been said, "Perceived confidence is almost as good as confidence." Can you also perceive yourself as confident by shifting how you carry and express yourself? Remember, you can't just think your way into a new way of feeling; you have to *act* your way into a new way of feeling.

Standing in a confident posture can boost how you feel about whatever new thing you are about to try. Likewise, when you practice *acting* confidently, even on your own, you can actually bring out more confidence and help *others* perceive you that way.

for you to do

Think of times when you go outside your comfort zone, and how your body sensations, stance, posture, and overall nonverbal behaviors affect you. Then answer the following questions:

Think of a time when you were about to do something new and unfamiliar. What sensations did you feel in your body? What thoughts ran through your head and claimed your attention?

_____

_____

_____

When you are unsure or nervous, what type of nonverbals might indicate you are unsure? Do you stand a certain way? Do you look down? Do you stand tall or hunch over?

_____

_____

_____

When feeling unsure about trying something new, consider moving your focus from your mind to your body. Instead of shrinking and looking at the floor, what might it be like to stand a little taller, feet planted firmly, head high?

_____

_____

_____

Try standing in a confident pose or posture: standing up, hands either on your hips like a superhero or above you, head and chest held high. Then try slumping over, like you're overwhelmed with self-doubt. How do you feel different in each of these poses, not just physically, but emotionally?

_____

_____

_____

Try standing tall like a tree, with your feet confidently planted on the floor. Mindfully press your feet into the ground and take a few minutes to notice all the sensations.

Sitting or standing, press your feet into the ground. Is the ground hard or soft, are your feet warm or cool, are your shoes tight or loose? Notice any other sensations. Gently press your feet into the floor beneath you, confidently rooting yourself like a tree.

What was it like to intentionally stand tall? What did you notice?

_____

_____

_____

When and where in your life do you think you could stand tall or use a confident pose to boost your confidence? You can do this in the bathroom or locker room; you do not have to do this on the sidelines or in your classroom! (If you are feeling ridiculous walking around like a superhero, just imagine yourself posing or moving confidently; that actually gives you some of the same effects.)

_____

_____

more to do

To not get stuck in a mind full of doubts, call on your inner ally from Activity 5. Your inner ally helps you be your best and roots for you always. With your best interests in mind, your inner ally brings out your courage and can help you act as confidently as you can, even if you don't feel 100-percent confident just yet. Your inner ally helps you face doubts with words of encouragement that can bring you compassionately back to belief in your own capabilities. For example, rather than focusing on how you don't know what you're doing (which of course would be normal when you're learning and putting yourself out there), your inner ally might say something like "Hey, this is just new. You're growing. Do your best and learn from this experience. You got this."

What might your inner ally say to you before you try something new to help you remember your capabilities even when you might be unsure? If you need extra help, go back to Activity 5 and try the Merging with Your Inner Ally meditation for extra inspiration.

_____

_____

_____

Some people like to imagine enlisting a team of allies when they are doing something new, standing behind them rooting for them when they feel unsure. (See the Squad of Kindness in activity 12.) What would your squad say to you when the fears came up?

_____

_____

_____

Your inner ally can help you get out of your head and into your body by working with your stance. Try this practice we call Puff Yourself Up.

First, notice how your body feels right now.

Start in a posture that signals low confidence, maybe slumping over in your seat. With each inhale, imagine you are breathing in confidence. For you that could be a certain color or an image: a lion, a mountain, a superhero. As you breathe in, imagine you are inflating yourself like a balloon, confidence filling out to your edges, so you sit or stand straighter and with more confidence. Imagine your inner ally cheering you on as you fill up with more strength and courage with each breath. Try it for about ten or twelve breaths, slowly puffing yourself up.

How does your body feel now?

_____

_____

_____

Do you notice any difference in your mind?

_____

_____

_____

Imagine times when you might try this practice. How might connecting with your inner ally and body (rather than focusing on nerves and worries) influence your confidence?

_____

_____

_____

Conclusion

We hope this section has helped you better identify challenging moments and triggers when your confidence fails you. The more of these you can identify, the more you can apply confidence boosts when you need it most. You may well find the practices are useful for all kinds of situations, not just the ones we focused on in this section. We hope you can practice all of these and find many places where they can work.

Write down a few of your favorite practices from part 2 and where you can imagine using them.

_____

_____

_____

_____

_____

PART 3

Social Life

Self-confidence can play a major role in your social life. It can help you make new friends, get involved, and be your best with others. This comes in handy when social fears arise in new places or with new people. Plus, a cushion of confidence helps you bounce back from social setbacks, so important in your teen years.

This part of the book tackles some of the most common social scenarios our clients bring up in therapy that tend to shake confidence. We explore how you can engage with your social world with more confidence, like when you need to put yourself out there, manage social anxiety, or establish healthy boundaries and confidently say no. We also get into how you can deal with public mistakes, uncertainty, and disappointments in your relationships.

We should mention that when it comes to social life, identity factors related to race, gender, sexual orientation, or ethnicity can leave you feeling like you don't belong, compounding your need for greater self-confidence. Maybe you feel like you just don't fit in. Regardless of the reason, if you feel like you're on the outside looking in, remember that a healthy relationship with yourself is more important than your social status. Working on *that* relationship, using some of the ideas in this section, will help you both navigate current social challenges and attract future connections that are right for you. So, regardless of your current relationships, don't lose faith. Stay curious, and explore this last section knowing that your social confidence can grow, and that growth will be a huge asset for forming healthy social relationships well into the future.

Social confidence can come up in various ways. For example, perhaps you don't feel confident because you haven't found a group you click with yet, or because you avoid social situations in general. Maybe you have positive social relationships but are unsure how to handle tricky dynamics of dating and friendships. Regardless of how social you are, we offer ideas and practices helpful for building social confidence—really, for anyone who has to deal with the tricky social dynamics that come with high school social life.

What are the areas where you could use more social confidence? What underlying issues might be impacting your social confidence? Are you more confident in some aspects of social life and could use a boost in others (say, dating, initiating friendships, feeling hurt by others, jealousy, or comparing yourself)?

getting out there

for you to know

How many times have parents or friends suggested that you "just put yourself out there more"? We remember receiving that profoundly unhelpful advice in our younger years. While it was well intentioned, we could never understand what exactly it meant, or how to even begin.

The way we see it is, you don't have to put yourself out there all at once. You can start small, really small, with confidence and work toward that bigger goal of doing what matters to you. By venturing out of your comfort zone (but well within your safety zone), you'll start meeting more people and getting more comfortable with putting yourself out there.

It's helpful to think about what's within your control and what's not. For example, you can't control other people, but you can learn to control yourself, to a certain extent, around other people. You can't control whether you have to go to school, do class presentations, or take tests, but you can start to have some power over how you manage these situations that are just a part of life.

for you to do

This means starting with some "radical acceptance": accepting that some things in life you just can't change, and letting go of the fight that's exhausting you. By stepping away from an unwinnable fight, you'll have the energy (and the confidence) to manage other situations in your life that matter more to you.

What are some things that you probably can't change? Think of social events, school expectations, your family, the world at large.

_____

_____

_____

_____

What are some ways you could change yourself in relation to these?

_____

_____

_____

_____

more to do

To go deeper with these concepts, we are inspired by a mindfulness-based therapy called acceptance and commitment therapy (ACT). The following helpful chart, the ACT Matrix (Polk & Schoendorff, 2014), helps you see more clearly how you usually respond to challenges and what you can do instead.

In box 1 (on the Moves Toward side), you'll write in some values and goals that matter to you—for example, to be more social, to feel comfortable singing onstage in front of a crowd, to at least try out for varsity whether you make it or not, to present your best self in a college or job interview.

Gabby's example appears first, showing that she wanted to move *toward* spending more time with friends and acquaintances.

In box 2 (on the Moves Away side), you'll write your internal blocks: what happens when you try these things or even *think* about trying them physically, emotionally, and psychologically? What are the thoughts, feelings, and impulses that move you *away* from what matters to you?

Gabby had a lot of anxiety and "what if" thoughts that came up just thinking about going to a party.

In box 3, you'll write the behavioral blocks that typically help you get rid of the internal discomfort. Do you avoid? Distract? Give up? Eat your lunch hiding in the library? Pick arguments you can't win?

Gabby was stuck in some big avoidant patterns that moved her *away* from what mattered to her. She said no to all invites and spent way too much time in her room.

Finally, in box 4, you'll write some small steps and actions that move you *toward* your goals and values. Maybe that's practicing something, signing up for tryouts, even talking to a friend about the goal. Maybe it's just smiling at that cute kid in the hallway, chatting in the cafeteria line about what horrors they are serving up today, or making another ordinary social gesture. Write down even the smallest things that might move you toward your goals.

Gabby was at a point where she was finally ready to say yes to an invite. She made a plan to go to her friend's party; she could see that even though it would feel uncomfortable, it would be a move toward what she wanted.

BEHAVIORAL BLOCKS: Behaviors I use to get rid of uncomfortable thoughts feelings Staying home, avoiding, saying no to invites, staying comfy in my room; making excuses; ignoring texts 3	ACTION PLAN: Small steps I can take TOWARD who and what is important Eat with friends for lunch and skip the library; go to Nico's party this weekend; reach out and respond to friends more 4
MOVES AWAY	**MOVES TOWARD**
INTERNAL BLOCKS: Uncomfortable thoughts + feelings Anxiety, jitters, "what if" thoughts, worries my friends will think I am quiet, worries I will panic if I go to party 2	VALUES: What's important and who matters to me Friends, family, making more time for people I love 1

Now fill in the blank matrix for a goal you want to move *toward*.

BEHAVIORAL BLOCKS: Behaviors I use to get rid of uncomfortable thoughts and feelings 3	ACTION PLAN: Small steps I can take TOWARD who and what is important 4
MOVES AWAY	**MOVES TOWARD**
INTERNAL BLOCKS: Uncomfortable thoughts + feelings 1	VALUES: What's important and who matters to me 2

Start thinking about the avoidant patterns you wrote in box 3 as moves *away* from what you want. What are your away moves? What pulls you away from your goals?

_____

_____

_____

_____

What *toward* moves are you ready to start (box 4)?

_____

_____

_____

_____

16 worries before you arrive

for you to know

Do you sometimes feel anxious when thinking about upcoming events or future experiences? That's part of the brain's job: to anticipate worst-case scenarios and plan accordingly, to keep you safe. But sometimes, when the brain creates those horror stories, you can lose confidence. This is called "anticipatory anxiety": anticipating or predicting that things won't go well before an event or experience, so much so that it actually hurts rather than helps. Often the worries before arrival feel much worse than whatever actually unfolds. Read about Gabby's anticipatory anxiety and see if you can relate.

On the way to Nico's party, Gabby wondered if she'd made a mistake saying she'd go. She originally wanted to, but on the way she got uneasy and nervous. Her body was tense and hot, and her heart began to race. She worried she was going to feel even worse at the party. She started to focus on the jittery sensations in her body, while the worst-case scenarios played out in her head. What if she was too quiet and shy? What if her friends regretted inviting her? What if they ignored her?

On top of her "what if" thoughts, her self-criticism jumped in to further crush her confidence. Now she was annoyed for feeling anxious in the first place and started to feel badly about herself. She wished she could be more chill and confident. The more she thought, judged herself, and focused on her discomfort, the more her anxiety and dread increased. She hated feeling anxious. She would rather be alone in the comfort of her room.

She quickly started trying to come up with excuses to get out of going. But then she remembered a recent conversation with her therapist. Gabby had admitted that she was tired of missing out. She didn't want to follow her classic avoidance pattern: making excuses to get out of invites and allowing anxiety to call the shots. She was sick of how her avoidance impacted her friendships and social life. Her therapist encouraged her to try to break the avoidance pattern and try something different, not only to face her fears but also to move toward more time with friends, an area of life Gabby was neglecting.

Her therapist explained that rather than falling into her old habits, Gabby could try to change the way she relates to the anxiety and self-criticism—maybe even welcome it, since it was going to show up anyway. At first Gabby was confused. Welcoming anxiety sounded like the opposite of what she'd want to do. However, Gabby knew her old ways were not working for her; they kept her away from what she wanted. Rather than turning her car around, she was ready to turn the tables on these old reactions and take back her power.

She used a practice her therapist had taught her to work with her anxiety in a new way. The practice made the anticipation a lot easier to deal with and helped her enter the party with a bit more confidence. Gabby also realized that she felt pretty comfortable during the actual party once she got past her anticipation anxiety. In fact, that worry didn't last very long and she settled in pretty soon after she arrived.

for you to do

Before she arrived at the party, Gabby used a meditation practice called "taking and sending." This meditation is adapted from an ancient compassion practice called Tonglen, now used by many all over the world. We offer specific directions here, but before you try it, let's understand what you're taking and sending. You *take* in your anxiety on your inhale, labeling and welcoming anxiety rather than avoiding and resisting it. On your exhale you imagine *sending* yourself what you need.

Gabby chose to send herself confidence. This helped her respond to her worries in a gentle, helpful way, rather than with judgment or harshness. In the last part, you offer the practice to the many other people in the world who might be in a similar situation and imagine sending them confidence. This part helps widen perspective and reminds us that we are not alone, even if it sometimes feels that way.

Now try taking and sending for yourself. (An audio version is available as a free tool at http://www.newharbinger.com/50492.)

Try This: Taking and Sending

In a place where you won't be disturbed, find a comfortable position.

1. **Brave Self:** Start by imagining the wisest and most confident version of yourself. Imagine yourself with an attitude of inner strength, one strong enough to allow fears to visit and pass. With this image in your mind, shift your attention to the rising and falling of your breath and find a slower pace than your normal breathing.

2. **Taking:** On your in-breath, imagine taking in the visiting anxiety. As you slowly inhale, say "anxiety" as if you are recognizing and naming it, even welcoming it. With your brave self in mind, imagine breathing anxiety into your heart, knowing you are strong enough to take it in.

3. **Sending**: On your out-breath, imagine sending confidence out to yourself. As you release a slow exhale, say "confidence." Imagine sending yourself calmness and ease from a peaceful heart. You can come up with a different word that works best for you, such as "calm" or "peace." Repeat this, taking and sending slowly a few more times. There's no rush. Take in anxiety on the inhale and send yourself confidence on the exhale.

4. **Widening Your Perspective:** Think about all the others who might be anxious at this moment. On your in-breath, imagine taking their anxiety into your heart, knowing you are strong enough to take it in. As your brave self slowly inhales, say "anxiety." On your out-breath, imagine sending out ease and confidence to all those who feel anxious at this moment, including yourself. As you slowly exhale, say the word "confidence" and imagine breathing confidence out to all who need it across the globe.

What did you notice after taking and sending?

_____

_____

_____

When could it be helpful for you to practice taking and sending?

_____

_____

_____

For the situation you picked, circle the word you might want to use for the inhale as you're taking, or write in another word that fits best.

anxiety   fear   worry   jitters   panic

discomfort   _____   _____

It helps to find a word that best conveys what you might need. Think about the situation you chose to try taking and sending about, and circle the word that might work best for your exhale, or write another word that represents what you need in a difficult moment.

calm   peace   confidence   tranquility   ease   serenity

comfort   _____   _____

zooming out of insecurities 17

for you to know

Earlier in this workbook we talked about the brain's negativity bias, and we're sure you can understand how your brain's tendency to focus on what's wrong can bring you down. Although this is about our brain's desire to keep us safe, it does make us tend to overlook the good, which is not so helpful for our happiness or self-image. What's more, this negativity bias can apply to how we look at ourselves, too—keeping us less confident and thinking we are less capable than we are.

Our negativity bias can be a bit like zooming in on a photo to the point it becomes out of focus, or so enlarged that you can only see the image's pixels. Pixels are essential to a photo, as they are the smallest item of information in a picture. However, sometimes when you zoom in too far, those little details are so magnified they distort your photo into a sea of blurry squares.

Similarly, by zooming in so closely on the negative, your brain can lead you to compromise the bigger picture and overlook the good. You can view almost anything in this pixelated way, including your situation or yourself, overly focusing on what you don't have or your weaknesses. This inaccurate view minimizes your strengths and compromises your self-confidence. Learning how to zoom out and see the bigger picture is an important skill not just for your well-being but also for how you feel about yourself and your experience.

It's important to know when you might be zooming in on negatives, seeing yourself and your life with a pixelated, blurry perspective. And it's important to know how to step back and zoom out, gaining a wider perspective to more effectively move through challenges rather than magnify them.

for you to do

Think back to a time when you might have zoomed too far in on the negatives. Read Alexandra's story, then answer the questions that follow and reflect on experiences where your narrow view negatively impacted your mood and confidence.

Alexandra reluctantly went on vacation with her family. She was upset that while she was away she would miss parties that a group of new friends had finally invited her to. She also worried that if she missed these, the invites from her new friends might slow down or stop. She'd just gotten to know these friends, and although things were going well, she'd had some bad social experiences at her old school that she didn't want to repeat. She wanted these new friendships to work out and was a little nervous they would somehow vanish while she was away.

Alexandra spent the first half of vacation sulking and checking her phone. She zoomed in on social fears to the point that her worries became exaggerated and unrealistic. She was so focused on worst-case scenarios with friends that the paradise that was right in front of her became pixelated and out of focus. So did the reality that her new friendships were not like past friendships; they were actually quite strong and healthy. Yet, as she zoomed in, she started to assume the worst about not getting instant replies to her texts. As she played out scenes of rejection in her mind, her perspective shrank further, and her insecurities grew and got the best of her.

In the middle of the trip, Alexandra posted a photo from a hike. A few of her new friends commented on the beautiful view and how Alexandra was lucky to be there. That's when Alexandra realized she hadn't fully seen how magical the view was until much later as she scrolled through her photos after the hike. And then it really hit her. She wasn't just missing out on parties with friends, who did appreciate her; she was also missing out on her own vacation—and the reality that her friendships were not as fragile as she'd feared. Her new friends weren't using her absence as a reason to shut her out in the future. In fact, they were happy to see photos from her vacation and looking forward to hearing more about it when she got back. Zooming in had distorted her lens.

Alexandra decided to shift her focus and bring more attention to the present instead of dwelling on her social standing. She made an effort to be more present on her trip and intentionally notice the beauty around her, and to check her phone less. All of this helped her find a balance: staying connected with friends and the present moment in front of her. As her perspective widened, she was able to enjoy the second half of her trip.

Think of a time in your life when, like Alexandra, you focused on what was wrong to the point that your perspective got a little pixelated and led you to miss the more positive aspects of your situation.

_____

_____

_____

_____

If you could go back, how could you have zoomed out and shifted your perspective? What might have helped to remind you to zoom out?

_____

_____

_____

Do you ever view yourself in a pixelated way? What weaknesses do you tend to zoom in on? What strengths do you tend to overlook?

_____

_____

_____

What could you do or say if you catch yourself zooming in on personal flaws and losing sight of the good in your life?

_____

_____

_____

_____

_____

_____

more to do

One helpful way to zoom out and disrupt the brain's negativity bias is to look for the good in the situations you're in—to practice gratitude. This will help your confidence, relationships, and resilience. Bringing gratitude into your life, appreciating what you have, is a proven way to boost your mood and well-being.

See if you can write three positives about your day for one full week. You can do this at whatever point in the day works best for you. Some people prefer the beginning of their day; others prefer bedtime. It's important to be consistent for one straight week, so try your best to identify three things you are grateful for each day for all seven days.

Of course, this can be hard on days that just aren't that great—which we all have sometimes. Keep in mind that this exercise is about noticing and looking for the good, no matter how small, or ordinary. Even something as simple as a good snuggle with your pet, a light homework day, or enjoying a drama-free day or class period is worth recording.

Day 1: Three Good Things   Date _____

    1. _____

    2. _____

    3. _____

Day 2: Three Good Things   Date _____

    1. _____

    2. _____

    3. _____

Day 3: Three Good Things   Date _____

   1. _____

   2. _____

   3. _____

Day 4: Three Good Things   Date _____

   1. _____

   2. _____

   3. _____

Day 5: Three Good Things   Date _____

   1. _____

   2. _____

   3. _____

Day 6: Three Good Things   Date _____

   1. _____

   2. _____

   3. _____

Day 7: Three Good Things   Date _____

   1. _____

   2. _____

   3. _____

Once you've done this consistently for a week, take time to reflect.

What was it like to intentionally be grateful for simple things? Was it difficult? Did it get easier over time? Did you notice any benefits to zooming out or looking for the good?

_____

_____

_____

_____

How could you keep up a gratitude practice? Could you find a partner to share three good things each day? Could you keep a gratitude journal, write a gratitude letter? What other ways can you think of to invite more gratitude into your life?

_____

_____

_____

_____

18 your comparing mind

for you to know

A surefire way to get down on yourself is by comparing yourself to others. It rarely goes well. Add the fact that the adolescent brain is more wired to compare itself to others than at any other life stage, marinate it all in social media, and soon enough anyone will look (and feel) terrible.

There's a self-help slogan we like: "Don't compare your insides to other people's outsides." We wish we'd heard this when we were younger! Still, even as adults Ashley and Chris can fall into the comparison trap, thinking everyone else is a better therapist or workbook writer than we are. But we've both learned to live with our comparing minds, and not buy into or get hooked by every depressing comparison our mind spits out.

Learning to shift your comparing mind can help calm down your threat system, rather than activate it, which ultimately benefits your well-being and confidence. To begin, simply notice and become more aware of your mind's tendency to compare. When you notice you're measuring yourself against a friend, you can say (internally or aloud) "comparing." This cues you to shift into a more helpful mindset, focused on your personal best, rather than trying to be "the best."

If you tend to rank and compare yourself a lot, especially unnecessarily, you are setting yourself up for chronic disappointment. There will always be others who have more, do better, and get further ahead. And that's actually okay once you realize that life is not one giant contest. It's more of a personal journey, which means all those comparisons aren't needed. What's more, letting go of comparisons allows us to be happy for others when they are winning, to see their win as a source of inspiration rather than a reason to take them down. Also, it's a lot easier to enjoy your personal journey when you aren't so worried about measuring up to someone else's. This is why people say "Comparison is the thief of joy."

for you to do

Reflect on the following questions to see how shifting out of your comparing mind could be helpful.

What are the most frequent comparisons you make about yourself? Who do you compare yourself to? What are some areas of your life where it might be helpful to catch yourself comparing?

_____

_____

_____

_____

_____

How might noticing and shifting your focus away from comparisons help your mood, relationships, and confidence?

_____

_____

_____

_____

_____

Even in areas of life where you might be competing, like in sports or class rankings (or social media attention), how might it be helpful to focus on your personal best, rather than focusing on how you measure up with peers?

_____

_____

_____

_____

Imagine going to a party where you will meet all new people. First go with a mindset focused on finding the most popular crowd and impressing them. You are highly focused on comparisons and where everyone ranks socially. Then change your focus: Imagine going to the same party with a mindset focused on developing new friendships and finding people you enjoy talking to. How do the different mindsets affect your behavior, interactions, feelings, and thoughts? Which feels better and might be more valuable?

_____

_____

_____

_____

_____

Are there any areas of your life where it might be helpful to notice when your mindset is a little closer to the ranking focus in the first scenario? What would be the benefit of shifting out of the ranking mindset? How could this affect your confidence?

_____

_____

_____

_____

_____

_____

_____

more to do

Take some time to practice appreciation for the confidence you do have! Brainstorm a few things you feel confident about in your life, and see what you come up with. Try to answer the following questions without comparing yourself to anyone else.

What do you feel confident about in terms of your appearance, clothes, fashion style, or tastes?

_____

_____

_____

What do you feel confident about in terms of your brain, skills, and smarts and arts?

_____

_____

_____

What friendships and relationships do you feel confident about?

_____

_____

_____

If you struggle to think of anything yourself, take some time to reflect on what others like about you, your work, your contributions to a team or group.

for you to know

When we hear teens complain about their comparing mind, most of them mention their online experience. Social media apps make it seem like everyone else is more popular, prettier, funnier, smarter, and better at everything than you are or at least get you focused on all that stuff. Scrolling through other people's posts can really crush your confidence, even after you've had a success.

And we get it: you're probably already sick of parents and other adults in your life telling you to get off your phone and just stay off social media. We also get that it's not that simple or easy. Look, it's not that easy for us, either, to take time away from social media, and we're grown-ups! But maybe you can start to be more mindfully aware of how social media impacts you. We know that awareness has helped a lot of our teen clients feel more confident, both online and off.

Consider limiting your social media times to certain times or places, like not right before bed or when you are feeling down. You don't have to stop your social media habits altogether to feel better, but you can start to change your relationship with your devices—and you might want to, once you learn how the apps are made and what they're trying to make you do.

Social media companies deliberately show you content that will get you to keep checking and/or to provoke big emotional reactions—big anger, big anxiety, big sadness, big jealousy, big excitement, or big laughs. They know what keeps you glued to your device. They also send you content that makes you want to go back for more—maybe it's more laughs and inspiration, but also more debates and conflict, trying to get that mic drop on the online debate you were having with your friend's uncle. And of course they want you to go back and check your likes so they can have your attention as much as possible and create online habits that some would say are addictive. Rather than the either/or of getting totally sucked in or getting rid of your devices, it can help to put some thought into how you want to use them, so it's *you* who are in charge of you, rather than random app developers who can easily steal your time.

for you to do

Maybe just reading about this right now, you're getting that urge to scroll! And you know what? Go ahead. Get out your phone or device. But first, write down how you feel now, before you start scrolling. We'll wait.

_____

_____

Okay, you're back. How do you feel after that session? Better—or worse? How does your body feel? How about your emotions? What else do you notice? Write it all down here.

_____

_____

_____

_____

Now pick up your phone or device again and scroll a little more slowly. Start to notice how *each* post makes you feel. What sensations and emotions come up with each update you see from friends or strangers or other accounts? How about your confidence? Which people or accounts boost your confidence, and which bring it down? Which just distract you, or maybe even provoke anxiety and anger? Why do you think that is? Take some time to write down what you notice here.

_____

_____

_____

_____

more to do

Answer the following questions to think about how you can create a more balanced, healthier online diet.

Take some time to think about how much you use your devices and social media. How much do you look at other accounts, compared to how much you are checking your own likes and shares and followers? How does that feel?

_____

_____

_____

Take a look at all the accounts that you follow. Reflect a bit more deeply on which ones bring you up, which bring you down, which ones pull you back in more than you'd like. Are there some you can unfollow or hide, even temporarily? Are there some you can add to bring more positivity, creativity, and inspiration? What kinds of healthy things do you want to add to your social media diet, and what "junk food" accounts do you want to limit or at least balance out?

_____

_____

_____

What specific accounts or content could I add that would be positive for me?

_____

_____

_____

What specific types of people or accounts can I limit that are unhealthy for me?

_____

_____

_____

Now think about your healthy and unhealthy online behaviors. With any diet, you can find ways to reduce temptation by setting boundaries around times and places. What are ways you could set limits? Maybe limit where you have your phone or keep it at certain times? In your bag rather than your pocket? Downstairs instead of up in your room? Maybe limit the times you have it close by? You can also use apps to block yourself when you are trying to focus or do a social media detox (also a healthy idea).

_____

_____

_____

_____

Think about why checking on likes grabs your attention. Why do you check likes, and how might this be unhelpful for your self-confidence? If checking on your likes relates to concerns about your popularity, ask yourself: _How popular am I with myself?_ Can you work toward feeling good about yourself, regardless of the likes online and off? How could you decrease your focus and reliance on likes and why might this be helpful?

_____

_____

_____

_____

Now let's say you don't want to change a thing right now about your online behavior. We understand—your social media diet might be for another day. Instead—as inspired by our friend Dr. Kelly Wilson—take a second to imagine that you live in a world where you can be exactly who you want to be, without any pressure to be perfect, or live up to some image, or deal with appearances and keeping up with others. In a world where you are free to fully be yourself, how would you act around others? What would you be doing? How would others feel around you? Allow yourself to wonder and see if there is anything that might inspire your real life.

_____

_____

_____

_____

_____

_____

20 social disappointments

for you to know

Friendships are an important source of happiness and joy. However, they also bring disappointments and upsets. Sometimes people let us down; other times relationships just don't work out the way we hoped. Whether we feel hurt in small or large ways, social upsets can sting and leave us with self-doubt. We can easily take the situation personally, which tends to impact our confidence and insecurities.

Jesse recently had a confidence shake-up after a tricky situation in her friend group. She had been feeling left out by someone in the group, and after some confusion, she could see it wasn't in her head. She tried to talk about it with her friends, but that didn't work. What made the hot-and-cold friend group harder was that Jesse started to think the exclusion must be her fault—that there must be something wrong with her. Finally, after careful reflection with her therapist and some trusted friends, she saw there were mean girl dynamics at play that were not her fault. She was being targeted, and she no longer wanted to be in a group with this dynamic. Jesse realized the friendship no longer felt good and needed some healthier boundaries. She came up with a plan to invest more time in healthier relationships that left her feeling positive and found ways to separate herself from friendships that left her confused and upset.

Jesse found ways to accept and cope with her feelings about the friendship loss and rejection, which got easier over time. There were still painful moments: When she ran into her old friend at lunch or saw her old group laughing together, she could still feel the hurt in her heart. As painful as it was, she grew from the situation and ended up feeling stronger and more confident.

Something that helped Jesse handle the tougher moments, the ones when she struggled with the hurt and loss, was the *self-compassion break*, a practice from Drs. Christopher Germer and Kristen Neff's Mindful Self-Compassion (MSC) training program (Neff & Germer, 2018). What's great about this informal practice is that it's designed to be used on the spot, in those difficult moments when you feel the hurt.

To practice your own self-compassion break, you first come up with three phrases, one for each component of Dr. Neff's unique definition of self-compassion: mindfulness, common humanity, and self-kindness. Then in moments of difficulty, you can offer yourself a supportive touch like a hand to your heart and repeat your three phrases. These phrases can help activate your parasympathetic nervous system—your soothing system (that green circle you learned about in Activity 2). And they can remind you to be compassionate and kind to yourself—especially in the moments when you're feeling hurt and not so confident.

for you to do

First, create your phrases using the following table. On the left, we explain each of the components of Dr. Neff's self-compassion in more detail. You will then see an example of a standard self-compassion phrase, next to the specific wording Jesse chose. On the far right of the table, write phrases in your own words that fit with mindfulness, common humanity, and self-kindness.

Creating Your Self-Compassion Break Phrases			
	Example Phrase	Jesse's Phrase	Your Phrase
Mindfulness: Simply being aware of your experience or difficulty	*This is a moment of discomfort.*	This is a tough moment.	
Common Humanity: Remembering you're not alone; everyone finds life hard	*These moments are part of everyone's life.*	Everybody experiences stuff like this.	
Self-Kindness: Treating yourself like a good friend who is going through a similar thing	*May I be kind to myself and give myself the compassion I need.*	Be a good friend to yourself right now.	

putting it all together

On the left are the three phrases Jesse used when she took her self-compassion break. Put your three phrases in the box on the right.

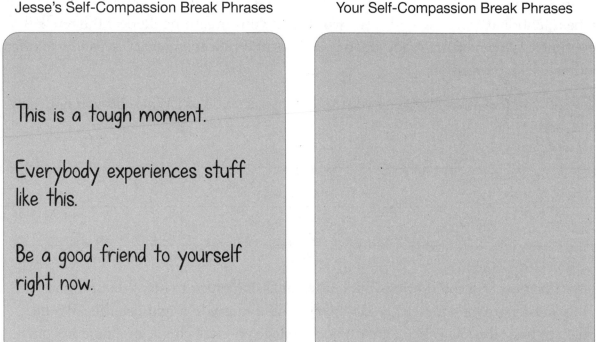

Jesse's Self-Compassion Break Phrases

This is a tough moment.

Everybody experiences stuff like this.

Be a good friend to yourself right now.

Your Self-Compassion Break Phrases

Jesse and her therapist used an app to make an image of her phrases. She saved the image to her phone and looked at it whenever she needed it most to remind herself to practice self-compassion. This gave her a strength and calm in moments where she felt down on herself. Anytime she saw herself slip into self-blame, she would put a hand on her heart, take a slow breath, and repeat the phrases to herself. This helped Jesse remember this was a difficult chapter, but it wasn't the end of her story.

more to do

Now to practice your self-compassion break. In a quiet setting where you won't be disturbed, close your eyes and put a supportive hand on your heart. Take a few breaths as you slow down your breathing. Next say your three phrases to yourself. Try to be intentional and slow with your words and your breathing. Repeat the phrases a few times. When you are ready, open your eyes and reflect on what it was like to offer yourself self-compassion.

How do you feel after practicing your self-compassion break? What did you notice in your body?

_____

_____

_____

Reflect on how you could bring your self-compassion break to life. What reminders will you prepare for yourself? And when are the times you might use this? Would it help to have this on a sticky note, a quote image on your phone, or a note in your planner? Maybe get it printed on a coffee mug?

_____

_____

_____

_____

_____

_____

for you to know

In Activity 20 we talked about those painful times when others let us down. Now we're doing a U-turn to tackle moments when we've let others down. We all make mistakes in life, and we all have choices about how to face the music. These choices can have a big influence, especially on our confidence and growth.

You can try to ignore mistakes, make excuses, or look away. This defensive, avoidant approach might seem good in the short run, but not for your relationships and growth in the long run. Or you could sink into the mistakes, falling into the quicksand of shame and self-criticism. This is also not so helpful because, as we learned in part 1, the shame-inner critic trap can sink your confidence.

A better strategy is to face the mistake but drop the harsh self-judgment. You can see the situation as an opportunity to learn and correct your error. This approach helps you not get so stuck in how bad you feel for yourself, and instead opens you up to how others feel as well. This matters because when you focus on "we," not just "me," you can see the bigger picture. From there you can find the right steps to repair and do better. What's more, this helps you move forward from social mess-ups with your confidence still intact.

So how can you do this? Simply patting yourself reassuringly on the back ("there, there") is clearly not going to cut it, because mistakes typically call for some type of honest feedback. And the inner critic loves to take over the feedback with lots of shame-based attacks. Unlike when the critic chimes in for no good reason, you might be more convinced when the critic uses your actual mistakes as proof of your badness. Dr. Dennis Tirch, a CFT and ACT psychologist, once shared an inspiring idea on this: "We have to give up the illusion of our specialness; we have to give up the specialness of our badness." We both like this idea, because in our offices we see firsthand how common it is for people to connect a bad choice with the "I'm a bad person" lament. It helps to watch out for this, because as Dr. Tirch reminds us, we are not each *uniquely* bad. We are simply human, with flaws and strengths being part of the deal.

Once you're aware of the inner critic and bad guy story getting in your way, then what? You need constructive feedback. And the way you deliver that feedback to yourself, including the tone you use, is key. This means knowing you are more than your worst mistakes, and righting your wrongs where you can.

There are some CFT concepts that can help us when we make mistakes. Essentially, instead of unhelpfully using *shame-based self-attack* (the fan favorite of the inner critic), you can address your mistakes constructively using *compassionate self-correction* (Gilbert, 2009). Compassionate self-correction taps into that voice of your inner ally, which helps activate the soothing system that can shift you out of threat. To see how this works, recall Jesse from the last activity, the one excluded from her friend group. There is actually a sequel to her story. Let's see how her friend Zoe shifted self-attack to compassionate self-correction when facing some regrets.

Although Jesse ultimately left the hot-and-cold friend group, she stayed friends with one of them, Zoe. Their friendship endured because Zoe was able to look at her own mistakes and shift her self-judgment to understanding. It started with Zoe asking Jesse why she had been so distant. Jesse explained how she felt hurt by her friends, including Zoe, over the last semester. Zoe was shocked, because she had never done anything directly. She was also initially a bit defensive; after all, she wasn't excluding Jesse and was just trying to stay out of the conflict. That evening, Zoe sat with her discomfort and started to feel ashamed about her silence, now seeing how that had played into Jesse's exclusion. What's more, she remembered a time when Jesse had brought it up and Zoe had dismissed her. She felt more empathy and compassion for her friend, then more regret that she'd been too busy to notice. She could see now that she could have done more, and she was disappointed in herself. As Zoe faced the discomfort of letting a good friend down, thoughts and feelings swirled. Her inner critic stepped in, telling her how selfish and mean she was. She even heard her critic say "This is the real you, not that nice girl you pretend to be." She noticed the bad guy story and how her inner critic was expanding her mistakes into some deeper meaning of who she really was.

Fortunately, Zoe caught the self-judgment. And instead of going along with either extreme—the critical-self attack or letting herself off the hook—she paused and shifted to a wiser voice, an inner ally that helped her understand what had happened and figure out actions to correct her wrongs. She realized she wasn't the upstanding friend she could have been because she had tried to be neutral, which just seemed safer when she lacked the necessary confidence. But she could now see how her silence made her complicit. With that understanding, she shifted her shame to guilt, which motivated her to action and the desire to do better. She wanted to be less of a bystander in the future and to handle her friend group more responsibly. She confidently called Jesse to apologize and own her part in the situation. Happily for both, Jesse accepted Zoe's apology, and they were able to restore their friendship. They walked away from the drama with a bit more wisdom and confidence, which came in handy for future relationships where they needed to set boundaries and speak up.

for you to do

Zoe could have easily let herself off the hook or sunk into shame. But instead of piling on, she shifted from judgment to understanding, which helped her get out of threat and find ways to make things right.

Read Zoe's inner critic and inner ally voices in the following chart and think about the differences between the two. To strengthen your inner ally's voice, think of any recent situations where, like Zoe, you needed to give yourself some corrective feedback. First fill in what your inner critic would say, on the left; then on the right, fill in what your inner ally might say to be more helpful.

INNER CRITIC	INNER ALLY
Critical Self-Attack	Compassionate Self-Correction
Your friend thinks you're terrible. And she's right. You pretend to be all nice and sweet, but this is the real you. Deep down, you're selfish and heartless. You only care about yourself.	Ouch. This is a difficult moment. Can you be less harsh with yourself right now and get through this? I'm with you. It makes sense that you don't feel great about these actions. This isn't how you want to treat others. At the time, you turned away from your friend, thinking it would be best to stay neutral. Now you can see your role and can do better moving forward. It sounds like you have some things to say to your friend. Even if she doesn't accept your apology, the right thing to do is to own your part and try to make things right where you can.

INNER CRITIC	INNER ALLY
Critical Self-Attack	Compassionate Self-Correction
What's the matter with you? How could you have done that to a friend? You saw the conflict brewing and did nothing. You knew she was being left out, and you didn't care. You're the worst! And you really don't deserve to be friends with Jesse.	This is upsetting. Letting someone down in this way hurts. There are times when we really miss the mark and have to learn. Let's find some words to express to your friend and think through ways where you might need to speak up more. We can find a way to try to course correct. Let's see how we can best get through the storm. I'm here for you.

more to do

Learning to speak to yourself with compassionate self-correction takes practice. Because it is so helpful to boost self-confidence and to shift out of threat, we encourage you to pay attention to your tone and inner feedback. To think a bit more about how and why this works, answer the following questions.

Jesse was able to give Zoe honest, constructive feedback, which helped Zoe hear the issues more willingly than she would have if she'd been shamed by her friend. Imagine if a coach, teacher, or friend gave you tough feedback in a constructive way, as Jesse did. In contrast, think of an opposite experience, in which you got feedback that was a bit harsh. What was the difference in delivery, and why was one more helpful than the other?

_____

_____

_____

Now think of a time when you had been feeling down and felt better after talking to a friend. What qualities of the supportive person helped you feel calmer after speaking with them? For example, did you walk away feeling understood, or judged?

_____

_____

_____

Next, contrast that with an experience where you reached out to someone who made you feel worse. Or think of someone you would never call if you're upset because you just know they would make you feel worse. What is it about the person who made you feel worse, or the one you would never call, that leads you to feel this way about them? Did they make you feel judged or criticized? Would they scold you with a harsh tone? Write about the differences in the responses and how they made you feel.

_____

_____

_____

_____

_____

We've learned that judgment and criticism activate our threat response, whereas understanding and caring activate a more calming response. This is why we feel better when loved ones give us compassion, and worse when someone judges us. In addition to having supportive friends in your life, there is great value in learning to treat yourself as a supportive friend would, especially in times of stress and mistakes. Can you see the benefit of making an effort to speak to yourself constructively, with more care and support? (Hint: Think about the red and green circles in Activity 2.) How would it help to shift from your inner critic's voice to your inner ally's? What might the costs be if you stick with the critic?

_____

_____

_____

_____

_____

22 uncertainty

for you to know

When we face unknowns in our social life (and in life in general), it's normal for uncomfortable feelings to arise. In fact, uncertainty typically leaves us with lots more fear than confidence. Even though we might not like it, uncertainty is part of the human adventure we can't avoid. So it makes sense to learn how to work with it rather than work against it.

Yet when we are facing the unknowns of life—such as when we don't know where we stand with someone, when we are waiting to hear back from others, or when future plans are all up in the air—it's common to make our troubles worse by turning on that old struggle switch. Then we spend time and energy struggling with things we can't change. Lamenting how we don't like the unknowns. Wishing we could make things more clear, when we can't. Trying to force answers, and sinking into frustration when none appear. As we struggle with this experience, we tend to feel worse. Sometimes we even try to feel better by unintentionally acting out in ways that create more trouble.

To turn off the struggle switch, we can meet the unknowns of life with an alternative, more helpful approach—an attitude of *allowing* and *letting be*. In mindfulness-based cognitive therapy, this is described as allowing space for whatever is going on, rather than trying to change your feeling or situation (Segal & Teasdale, 2013). This doesn't mean action and change are not valuable too; rather, it means first taking a moment to be more aware of our inner world and allowing unwanted sensations and experiences to just be. When we do this, we find we can actually face the unknown from a place of clarity, patience, and confidence—instead of letting it set us back and drive us to self-sabotage.

for you to do

We recognize that allowing is not the easiest concept to grasp. To illustrate, imagine the following scenario:

Imagine you can have a party and invite anyone you want. You are in complete control of the guest list, and it turns out everyone you invite can attend. But pretend there is one small, magical catch: before your party can start, you must first welcome and be friendly to some uninvited guests that you have zero desire to ever be around.

Why, you ask? Well, we'll explain in a minute; for now, try to just go with it.

You first try to think of clever ways to get out of dealing with the uninvited. You try to hide out in your room, but they only stay longer, and now you are trapped in your room and you don't get to see your friends. So next, you leave your room and try to ignore the uninvited people. But they get louder and try to get your attention in more obnoxious ways.

After all your effort to avoid and resist, you decide to finally greet these guests and stop fighting their presence. You remind yourself this is just a visit; they aren't moving in. It turns out your strategy to accept rather than resist the guests was effective. They liked being acknowledged, and they left pretty quickly. When you stopped trying to change the situation and started allowing and letting be, your situation greatly improved: the unwelcome visitors passed through, and you went on to enjoy your invited guests.

The uninvited guests in this scenario are the uncomfortable feelings and experiences that visit us throughout our lives, especially in uncertain times. As humans, we all have these guests, and many of us hit the struggle switch on without much awareness. But sometimes our best response is to change our automatic struggle and instead allow and let be.

What might be some benefits of making room for uncertainty and accepting unwanted feelings? How could this affect your confidence and coping? Hint: Think about the party story—the negatives of trying to avoid the unwanted guests, and the positives of accepting them.

_____

_____

_____

_____

_____

more to do

Read about how Rafael made space for his feelings and moved through uncertainty with confidence. Then answer the reflection questions to see how you might apply this to your life.

Rafael was excited about the potential of dating Sofia. She seemed interested, and there was a good flow to their communication. But then the messaging started to slow down a bit. One weekend he finally got the nerve to ask her out but was stuck waiting for her reply. The uncertainty started to get uncomfortable, and his confidence was getting shaky. Though he knew he should wait for her to reply, the unknowns got to him. Trying to get some answers, he started writing Sofia a message he would surely regret.

Instead of hitting send, Rafael paused. He knew he was about to sabotage things; the multiple nagging messages weren't a good look and could push her away. In a mindfulness class, he had recently learned about allowing, and he thought letting things be would be a better move. As he felt the pull to seek reassurance from Sofia and reach out again, he reflected on how he was feeling in that moment. Rafael took a few breaths and intentionally focused on the difficulty of the situation. He allowed himself to admit that he was anxious and didn't like all the unknowns in the dating process. Then he focused on where he was feeling the sensations in his body. He deliberately brought attention to his chest, where he was feeling it the most. He repeated, "Allow and let be. I can handle not knowing."

After this pause, he felt better. He could see that sending another text was a reaction to anxiety and he didn't have to follow anxiety's demands. He realized the wise move would be to not send the text; to wait, rather than trying to force things. He felt more at ease and confident with the situation, even though it was still unclear. Just like with many other questions in life, he trusted that in time, things would be clear. As he waited, he made plans with friends, put limits on how much he focused on the anxious thoughts, and spent time doing things that mattered to him. Eventually his relationship with Sofia did grow stronger and it was clear where they stood with each other. He went on to feel more confident in his new relationship and in his ability to patiently navigate the unknowns.

Consciously pausing and allowing helped Rafael to be with his feelings with more ease without getting lost in them. What did Rafael specifically do (and not do) to create an allowing attitude to his feelings and situation?

_____

_____

_____

_____

_____

When might it be helpful for you to try Rafael's allowing approach in your life?

_____

_____

_____

_____

_____

Rafael's first approach to his discomfort had been to text Sofia for reassurance, but he'd realized that was just an unhelpful attempt to make his anxiety go away, which could backfire. Can you identify any unhelpful ways you might push away unwanted feelings? In the following list, check any you might be using. Feel free to add to the list.

Avoiding Unwanted Feelings and Experiences

☐ Refuse to talk or acknowledge feelings.

☐ Zone out.

☐ Play video games and ignore the difficulty.

☐ Spend more time than you want to on social media.

☐ Get overly busy or overly focused on tasks.

☐ Drink or use substances.

☐ Blame others.

☐ Focus on how unfair it is to feel this way.

☐ Distract yourself by doing anything other than what you are supposed to do.

☐ Try to control the situation in a way that doesn't help.

☐ Repeatedly seek reassurance from others.

☐ Try to problem solve something that can't yet be solved.

☐ _____

☐ _____

☐ _____

Here are some more helpful ideas that can allow you to make space for uncomfortable feelings. Look through the list and check ones you might use. Feel free to add to the list and write about how you might want to meet your next unwanted moment.

Allowing Unwanted Feelings and Experiences

- ☐ Write in your journal.

- ☐ Take the time to label your feelings.

- ☐ Talk to someone you trust about your feelings.

- ☐ Remind yourself that feelings are visitors and this is part of the human experience.

- ☐ Practice 3-6-9 Breathing (Activity 2).

- ☐ Practice the Mindful SEAT (Activity 8).

- ☐ Try the Taking and Sending Practice (in Activity 16).

- ☐ Take a Self-Compassion Break (in Activity 20).

- ☐ Try to be curious rather than judgmental about your feelings.

- ☐ Notice where you feel the emotion in your body and repeat "Allow and let be."

- ☐ Shift your attention to your breathing and your body sensations.

- ☐ _____

- ☐ _____

- ☐ _____

- ☐ _____

Rafael accepted that things would be uncertain with Sofia for a bit and he would need to be patient. It helped him to repeat "Allow and let be. I can handle not knowing." Thinking about any uncertain situations in your life, is there anything that might be helpful to accept? Are there any other phrases that might work for you?

_____

_____

_____

_____

_____

_____

Conclusion

We hope this final section, on social confidence, can help you—even just a little bit—to put yourself out there. We've explored some of the more common social scenarios and situations where confidence can crumble but mindfulness can lift us up, and we hope you'll have a chance to practice some of these ideas in those situations.

Still, life—and especially growing up—means unpredictable situations will find you. Life will be full of pop quizzes, curveball interview questions, new roommates, and even bigger surprises that you can't plan for. Many of the basics you've learned in these specific scenarios can help you in the tricky situations and unknowns that lie ahead.

Take some time to reflect on what exercises you found most helpful in this social life section, then consider when you might be able to use the basic principles at other times you need some confidence.

_____

_____

_____

_____

_____

Our hope is that you have found this book empowering for your confidence and self-knowledge. We hope you've discovered some of the roots of your confidence challenges and learned different ways you can boost your confidence over the short and long term and in situations where it used to sink. We hope, too, you have realized that you are not alone—not only are there millions of other teens with confidence lower than they'd like, but there are also millions who have learned how to boost and build their confidence. We further hope that you have found adults, peers, and friends you can share your wins and challenges with, who are there to support you in your growth and remind you of the confidence and capability that you do have, despite your inner critic.

With that, we encourage you to take a few moments to review and reflect on your favorite exercises from all three sections of this book, then identify those you want to use in challenging times. Feel free to reference your green circle in Activity 2 and list favorite practices throughout the book that can activate your soothing system and help you meet your confidence goals.

_____

_____

_____

_____

_____

_____

As a last practice, let's try something to get you moving—yes, very literally. This closing practice was inspired by a walking meditation we learned together in a mindful self-compassion class. We offer it to you to end this workbook and welcome healthy new beginnings into your next adventures.

Stand up, and feel the soles of your feet grounded in the earth beneath you, both grounding you and holding you up with the confidence you need.

Now begin to walk slowly forward, feeling the sensations of each footstep on the ground beneath you.

With each lifted foot, consider what you wish to leave behind you—perhaps doubt, uncertainty, fear.

And with each foot stepping down and moving forward, consider what you are walking toward—perhaps confidence, relief, relaxation.

Find whatever words, images, and qualities resonate for you as you continue to slowly walk forward, noticing the touch of your feet to the ground and inviting in confidence with each step.

As you leave imprints of strength behind, think of all those who are rooting for you on this journey into confidence.

When you are ready, come back to a standing position. Take a few moments to notice the sensations in your body. Allow yourself to feel whatever you may feel. As you go on to move through your day, may you stay grounded with strength and a steady heart.

In gratitude,

Ashley and Chris

references

Dweck, C. S. 2007. *Mindset: The New Psychology of Success.* New York: Ballantine Books.

Gilbert, P. 2009. *The Compassionate Mind.* London: Little, Brown Book Group.

Gilbert, P. 2022. "Shame, Humiliation, Guilt and Social Status: The Distress and Harms of Social Disconnection." In *Compassion Focused Therapy: Clinical Practice and Applications,* edited by Paul Gilbert and Gregoris Simos. London and New York: Routledge Taylor and Francis Group.

Kolts, R. L. 2016. *CFT Made Simple.* Oakland, CA: New Harbinger Publications.

Kolts, R. L., & Chodron, T. 2015. *An Open-Hearted Life.* Boulder, CO: Shambhala Publications.

Neff, K., & Germer, C. 2018. *The Mindful Self-Compassion Workbook: A Proven Way to Accept Yourself, Build Inner Strength, and Thrive.* New York, London: Guilford Press.

Polk, K. L., & Schoendorff, B. 2014. *The ACT Matrix: A New Approach to Building Psychological Flexibility Across Settings and Populations.* Oakland, CA: Context Press.

Segal, Z., Williams, M., & Teasdale, J. 2013. *Mindfulness-Based Cognitive Therapy for Depression* (2nd ed.). New York, London: Guilford Press.

Ashley Vigil-Otero, PsyD, is a psychologist in private practice, an author, and a consultant at the National Institute for the Clinical Application of Behavioral Medicine (NICABM). She has trained at Harvard Medical School and Vanderbilt University, and has taught at the University of South Florida. She practices in Florida, where she specializes in compassion-oriented psychotherapy with clients throughout the lifespan. Raised in a multicultural family, she has long-standing interests in cultural humility and diversity in mental health.

Christopher Willard, PsyD, is a clinical psychologist, author, and consultant based in Massachusetts. He has spoken in thirty countries, and has presented at two TEDx events. Willard is author and coauthor of twenty books, including *Alphabreaths*, *Growing Up Mindful*, and *How We Grow Through What We Go Through*. His thoughts on mental health have been featured in *The New York Times*, *The Washington Post*, www.mindful.org, www.cnn.com, and elsewhere. He teaches at Harvard Medical School.